THE VICTORIA HISTORY OF HAMPSHIRE

STEVENTON

Jean Morrin

with contributions by John Hare

First published 2016

A Victoria County History publication

© The University of London, 2016

ISBN 978-1-909646-21-6

INSTITUTE OF HISTORICAL RESEARCH | University of London School of Advanced Study

Cover image: St Nicholas church, Steventon, before the Victorian restoration and as Jane Austen saw it. (© Winchester Cathedral)
Back cover image: Memorial plaque dedicated to Jane Austen, resident of Steventon for 25 years. (Photograph by John Hare)

Typeset in Minion Pro by Jessica Davies

CONTENTS

LIST OF ILLUSTRATIONS

Photographs were taken by John Hare and Chris Morrin (unless otherwise stated) and are reproduced with their kind permission.

All maps are reproduced by permission of Hampshire Record Office unless otherwise stated.

Map

FOREWORD

THE IDEA OF a national series of town and parish histories for every county in England was first mooted at Queen Victoria's Diamond Jubilee in 1897 and the Victoria County History (VCH) was dedicated to her. In 2012, Her Majesty the Queen agreed to the rededication of the project to mark her own Diamond Jubilee.

Hampshire was the first county to publish a history of each of its parishes in red book volumes (1912) but these included only leading families, the Church of England and local charities. In 2008 Hampshire also became the first county to undertake a complete revision in the modern VCH style which includes the social, economic and religious history of the ordinary people of each parish. This is a voluntary project, led by professional historians, which has initially focused on Basingstoke and its surrounding villages. It is funded by donations from supporters and book sales. Ultimately a new red book series for Hampshire will appear but in the meantime, the Victoria County History, based at the University of London, is also publishing this series of individual and more in-depth parish histories, called Shorts, of which VCH Hampshire's *Mapledurwell* by John Hare, Jean Morrin and the late Stan Waight (2012) was the first to appear.

Steventon by Jean Morrin with contributions from John Hare is the second Hampshire publication in this new Victoria County History series. Steventon is famous for being the birthplace of Jane Austen, and both the influence of the village on her writing and her depiction of local society are discussed in this book. The parish history has other fascinating aspects such as the unscrupulous behavior shown by one of the lords of the manor in the late 16th and early 17th century. Detailed analysis of farming on the chalk lands is facilitated by the strength of the archive of the Knight family, who held the manorial lordship during the 18th and 19th centuries.

I commend this readable and scholarly parish history to you. Many more parish histories will follow as the research proceeds. I urge readers who enjoy this book to support the new VCH Hampshire project.

Nigel Atkinson Esq
HM Lord-Lieutenant of Hampshire

ACKNOWLEDGEMENTS

THIS PARISH HISTORY IS the second Short by the new Victoria County History of Hampshire which aims to rewrite the Hampshire volumes published a century ago. Publishing individual parish histories is designed to share the research of the project long before the planned new series of red books is ready for publication. Steventon was initially selected for publication as it was the birthplace of Jane Austen and her home for the first 25 years of her life, but the village is not as well known as Chawton, where her house is now a museum, or Bath with its famous Jane Austen centre. Steventon is also an example of a chalkland parish such as occurred throughout so much of Hampshire. Study of this parish is enhanced by particularly rich archival deposits. That of the Knight family, lords of the manor of Steventon from 1707 to 1855, deposited at Hampshire Record Office, the custodian of much of the documentation used, reveals how reforming, but non-resident private landlords, successfully managed the estate. Legal case papers, deposited in The National Archives, document the surprising crimes of one of the lords of the manor (1584–1611). Finally, Jane Austen's own letters tell us much about village society of her time.

This book owes a great deal to the VCH Hampshire team. John Hare has written the medieval and building sections, contributed to the introduction and given invaluable help with editing all the text. Mary Oliver wrote the archaeology section. Jennie Butler photographed many maps, plans and documents. Alison Deveson advised on Methodism. Joyce Bown, Geoff Mann and Richard Tanner provided local information. Wills and inventories relating to Steventon were transcribed by the wills group which meets regularly in Basingstoke and many Hampshire volunteers have read and commented on the text. The late Stan Waight drew the draft parish maps, John Hare and Chris Morrin photographed the parish landscape and buildings. Staff from the Hampshire Record Office have been very supportive of the project. Financial help has come from the Mark Fitch Fund, Charlotte Bonham-Carter Charitable Fund, The Bulldog Fund, University of Winchester, the Jane Austen Society and individuals, especially Professor Jim and Mrs Mary Ann Wilkes. We are most grateful to all for their support.

Guidance from Richard Hoyle's team at VCH central office at the Institute of Historical Research (University of London) has been invaluable, especially from Adam Chapman who helped to revise the manorial chapter and Jessica Davies who managed the production of the publication.

INTRODUCTION

THE SMALL RURAL PARISH of Steventon shows many of the characteristics of other southern chalkland settlements. It is located on the North Downs, near the source of the river Test, with Basingstoke, the nearest town, eight miles away to the north-east. The village economy until the 20th century was dominated by sheep and grain farming. The medieval open fields in the north of the parish were surrounded by chalk downland pastures, which over the centuries were inclosed. In 1512 open fields and inclosed fields co-existed, but in 1741 the remnants of the former disappeared.[1] From the Middle Ages until 1986 most of the parish was owned by successive lords of the manor, many of whom were absentee. One who was resident, Sir Pexall Brocas (1584–1611), achieved notoriety, disturbed the peace of the parish and was eventually driven out by his son, Thomas. The Knight family of Chawton (Hants.) and Godmersham (Kent), owned the manor from 1707 to 1855 and, although absentees, were active and reforming landlords. Thomas Knight commissioned maps of the parish, drawn by his steward, Edward Randell, in 1741 which are of great value as they depicted the settlement, roads and farms and fields including the last surviving open fields (Maps 5, 8, 10, 11 and 12).[2] Until 1841 Steventon was a detached part of Basingstoke hundred: an historic remnant of the old unit of government. It was separated from its neighbouring villages, which in the Middle Ages had all belonged to either the bishop of Winchester or the cathedral priory. After 1841, it was part of Overton Hundred, by which it was totally surrounded.[3] In 2015 it was part of the Borough of Basingstoke and Deane.

What has made the village well-known to a much wider audience, however, was the product of an accident of birth, for it was here that Jane Austen was born and grew up, her father having been presented to the parish as rector because he was related to the Knight family. No house or museum commemorates the author's memory in the parish where she spent her first 25 years (December 1775 to January 1801)[4] but it was 'the cradle of her genius', according to James Edward Austen-Leigh, her nephew (born 17 November 1798) and biographer.[5] Austen-Leigh argued that it was 'at Steventon that the real foundation of her fame was laid',[6] as family life and observation of north Hampshire society shaped her early literary career. She wrote early versions of *Pride and Prejudice*, *Sense and Sensibility* and *Northanger Abbey* in Steventon from 1796 to 1798. Her *Letters* shed light on some aspects of village life during this period.[7]

1   TNA, E 368/438; HRO, 39M89/E/B384/16.
2   Ibid., 18M61/MP22; 39M89/E/B384/16 and 17.
3   Youngs, *Admin. Units* I, 223.
4   HRO, 71M82.
5   Austen-Leigh, *Memoir*, 22.
6   Ibid., 47.
7   Austen, *Letters*.

In 2015 the parish had two centres: firstly, the church and manor house on a hill
adjoining the eastern boundary of the parish, which may also have been the site of the
earliest medieval village. The second formed a linear pattern along the western side
of the village street extending from Hatch Gate to the open space of the Triangle, and
then north to the railway embankment on the lane to Deane Gate, where there was also
some small-scale settlement (Map 1). Until c.1824 a third area of settlement extended
east of the Triangle to the old rectory, where Jane Austen was born (Maps 5, 13 and Fig.
24). Until the 20th century the workforce had been largely engaged in agriculture, but
in 2015, while it remained a rural village, most inhabitants commuted or worked from
home.[8] From 1986 the great estate was broken up and only a few farms survived.

Parish Boundaries

At the close of the 19th century, Steventon ancient parish covered 2,155 a. (Map 1).[9]
The parish formed a long narrow block, typical of many chalkland parishes. It ran
north-south with an almost circular bite out of it at the north-west end (Map 1). The
bite allowed all the Ashe Park estate, belonging to Ashe Park House (built very near to
the parish boundary, probably in the 17th century and rebuilt in 1865[10]) to be united
within the parish of Ashe. The parish boundaries mostly followed lanes or tracks and
field or wood edges but the northern boundary with Deane parish bordered the Andover
to Basingstoke turnpike road (constructed 1755) at Deane Gate.[11] The boundary then
ran south-east along field edges separating it from Oakley parish. It then turned south
and followed the edges of Stubbs Copse and West Wood in North Waltham parish as
far as the manor house and church on the far eastern edge of the parish.[12] From there,
the boundary crossed Waltham Lane, leading from Hatch Gate to North Waltham, and
followed field edges and Misholt Copse until it reached the north side of the Basingstoke
to Stockbridge turnpike road constructed in 1756 (A303 in 2015) in the south-east
corner of the parish.[13] The southern boundary then turned north-west away from the
road to run along the northern edge of Cocksford Down and Sheepdown Copse in
Popham parish, before turning sharply north then west around two sides of a field to
Beggar's Clump, from where it ran along the eastern edge of Burley Lane (Map 1) with
Popham Beacons to the west. The boundary then turned east towards Warren Farm,
north-west to Litchfield Grange and then north along narrow tracks on field edges,
including, in the north-west of the parish, those on the edges of the site of the last three
open fields. North and east of the old open fields was the large section of Ashe Park in
Ashe parish cut into Steventon parish. After this the boundary ran north to Deane Gate.

Minor changes to the parish boundaries were made in the 20th century including
the removal of the Ashe Park bite. In 1932 the boundary was altered to remove most of
the bite (105 a.) from Ashe to Steventon parish.[14] The new boundary followed the edges

8   See pp. 37–8.
9   OS Area Bk (1873).
10   *VCH Hants.* IV, 200.
11   Public Act, 28 George II, c.44.
12   OS Map 1:10560, Hants. XXV (1873 edn).
13   Public Act, 29 George II, c.46.
14   OS Map 1:2500, sheet 17.6 (1942 edn); OS 31/545 Boundary Map Revision of 1942.

Figure 1 *The southern boundary of the parish with Popham Airfield in the foreground and garages alongside the A303 boundary of the parish in the background.*

of a number of narrow fields which lay immediately east of the lane from Deane Gate to the Triangle. Ashe Park Farm was thus included in Steventon, while Kimber's Copse and Ashe Park House remained in Ashe parish.[15] A narrow section of Ashe parish still ran south from Kimber's Copse to the Firs and nearly to the railway embankment.[16] This boundary was altered again in 1985 to include all of Ashe Park in Steventon.[17] In addition at the same time, but on the opposite or southern edge of the parish, the boundary was moved south of Cocksford Down to adjoin the northern edge of the Basingstoke to Stockbridge road (A303), as this had become a major route which joined the M3 motorway, cutting off the northern part of Popham from the rest of the parish.[18] This change meant Popham Airfield was transferred to Steventon parish. The south-western tip of the parish was also extended by one field to run in a north-easterly direction to Beggar's Clump along Burley Lane. These 20th-century boundary changes increased the parish area to 2,456 a.[19]

Landscape

The parish is a long narrow strip, three miles long by one mile wide, lying on the North Downs. The underlying geology is entirely Upper Chalk with small thin drift deposits of clay with flints. There is clayey loam on the two dry valley floors (Map 2): one of which meanders north from Warren Farm to the Triangle with its southern end under the modern village street; the other extends along the lane from North Waltham to the

15 *London Gaz.*, 23 March 1928, 2116–18.
16 HRO, H/CL6/2/17/4.
17 Basingstoke and Deane (Parishes) Order 1985, Schedule 2; OS Map 1:25000, sheet 144 (Explorer, 2005 edn).
18 Ibid.
19 Generalised Land Use Database, http://www.neighbourhood.statistics.gov.uk (accessed Oct. 2015).

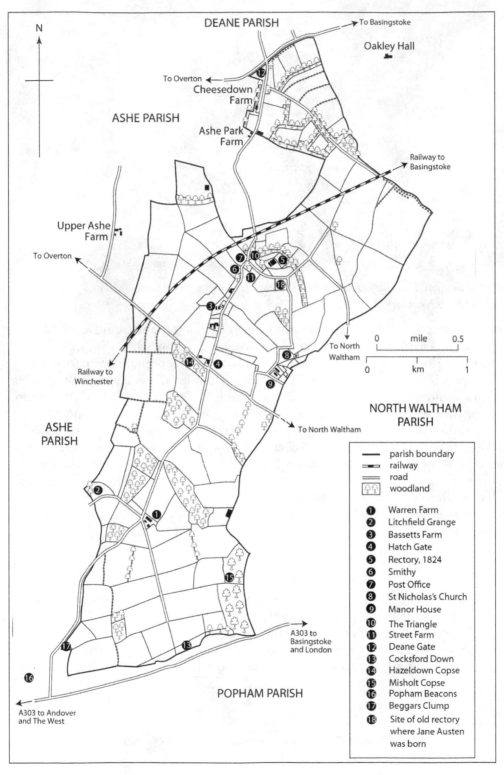

Map 1 *Steventon in 1871.*

Figure 2 *Arable fields and woods on the hill below the church in 2014.*

site of the old rectory (demolished 1824) and then is under the damp narrow lane from the rectory to the Triangle, where most of the village cottages stood in the 18th and early 19th centuries (Map 2).[20] The village settlement is small and sited in the northern sector of the parish, which since 1840 has been dominated by the high and substantial railway embankment (*c.*20 m. above the surrounding land) occupying 24 a. supporting the London to Southampton railway line (Map 7).[21] The ground at the Triangle, the centre of the settlement, is 102 m. high. In the 16th century open fields surrounded the village to the west, south and east[22] but these were inclosed in piecemeal fashion until 1741 when the last three fields, lying on a steep upward slope to the west of the village street, were inclosed (Fig. 3).

In 2015, arable and pasture land were mixed with woodlands (Fig. 2). Numerous old chalk pits, dug for agricultural use to spread and mix with the clay, were scattered around the parish.[23] In the absence of a stream, before the 20th century, water was taken from farm ponds, wells and springs.

The land rises gently over the downs to the south, especially south of Warren Farm, reaching a peak of 175 m. near its southern boundary on Cocksford Down. There are substantial woods in the southern part of the parish. The extensive open downland pastures to the south of the open fields were gradually encroached on by inclosure for

20   OS Map 1:50000 (Geological edn, 1972).
21   HRO, 21M65/F7/223/1.
22   TNA, E 368/438.
23   OS Map 1:2500 (1873 edn), sheets 17 and 25.

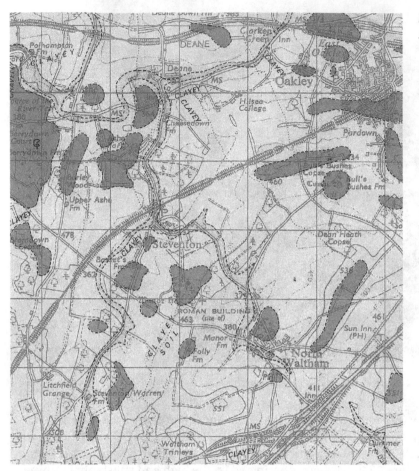

Map 2 *Geological map showing dry valleys.*

pasture and arable, probably during two periods of demographic expansion in the 13th century, as with Litchfield Grange, and in the 16th, as in the activity of Pexall Brocas.[24] Thus by 1741 the landscape of the south of the parish already comprised irregular closes of arable and rough pasture with some woodland. A lane ran through the rough pasture to the southern boundary (Map 3). What is not clear is when this pre-1741 field pattern came into being. Such piecemeal inclosure of the downs could have been medieval or post-medieval colonisation of hitherto uncultivated land. For much of the medieval period the downs were probably still open. This area was transformed from 1805 to 1840 by the development of Steventon Warren farm, to the south and east of Warren pond (Map 4).[25] As the farm developed, the fields were converted into square, regular shapes resembling those of Parliamentary Inclosure,[26] with a new straight road through the centre of the parish, leading to the Basingstoke to Stockbridge turnpike road (A303). The 77 a. of rough pasture and bushes through which the lane originally ran were grubbed

24   See p. 40.
25   HRO, 18M61/E. K. 2/box 2/bundle 20. See maps HRO, 39M89/E/B384/16 and 21M65/F7/223/1.
26   J. Chapman and S. Seeliger, *A Guide to Enclosure in Hampshire, 1700–1900* (HRS 15, 1997).

Figure 3 *Site in 2014 of the last open fields which were inclosed c.1741 with the railway embankment in the distance.*

up and converted into arable fields (60 a.) and woods (17 a.).[27] From Warren Farm a new road ran west then south to Litchfield Grange, a freehold farm on the western boundary, with a small wood, called Beggar's Clump, in the south-western point of the parish. The southern boundary change of 1985 transferred Popham Airfield, a private leisure facility, which serves as a base for owners of light aircraft or microlights, comprising two airstrips on Cocksford Down, to Steventon parish (Fig. 1). It had been established in Popham parish in 1975 when Charles Church (d. 1989) purchased the wooded area and organized clearance of the land. In 2014 the airfield was still owned by the family of Charles Church and was the home of the Spitfire Flying Club which had over 400 members. Companies offering flying training and aircraft maintenance were also accommodated on the site.[28]

Communications

Roads

Steventon lies between two main roads. Steventon's northern boundary at Deane Gate borders the old turnpike road from Andover to Basingstoke (built 1755, B3400 in 2015).[29] A listed, but damaged, milestone survives in the far north-west of the parish.[30] The Stockbridge to Basingstoke turnpike road (A303 in 2015) ran along the southern boundary of the parish. From 1985 the A303 joined the motorway (M3) south-east of Steventon.[31] The roads within the parish are all narrow lanes. A lane runs south from Deane Gate which from 1840 narrowed to pass under the railway embankment (Fig.

27   HRO, 39M89/E/B/384; 21M65/F7/223/1.
28   http://www.popham-airfield.co.uk (accessed 6 Apr. 2014).
29   HRO, 5M52/TR5; Public Act, 28 George II, c.44.
30   NHL, no. 1096169, 'Milestone on B3400 at approximately NGR 541 498' (19 Oct. 2015).
31   Public Act, 29 George II, c.46.

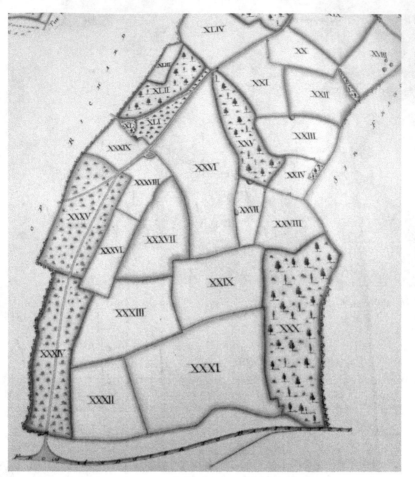

Map 3 *South Steventon in 1741 showing irregular fields and lane running through the rough ground.*

4) at Steventon Arch, to the Triangle. South of the Triangle, the village street extends to the cross roads at Hatch Gate and as a narrow lane to Steventon Warren, after which it joins Burley Lane from Ashe before reaching the southern boundary with Popham and the Andover to Basingstoke Road (A303). From Hatch Gate crossroads, Waltham Lane runs south-east to North Waltham where it becomes Popham Lane which leads to the Winchester to Basingstoke and London road (A30). In the late 18th century Jane Austen frequently noted the difficulty of travelling in and from Steventon in wet weather because of the muddy state of the lanes.[32]

Railway

The railway embankment (Fig. 4 and Map 7) on the London to Southampton railway dominates the north of the parish but there has never been a station in Steventon. In 2015, the nearest railway stations were at Overton, three miles north of Steventon, on the Basingstoke to Salisbury line, opened by the London & South Western Railway (L&SWR) in 1854 and Micheldever station, five miles from Steventon, and two and a half miles

32   Austen, *Letters*, passim.

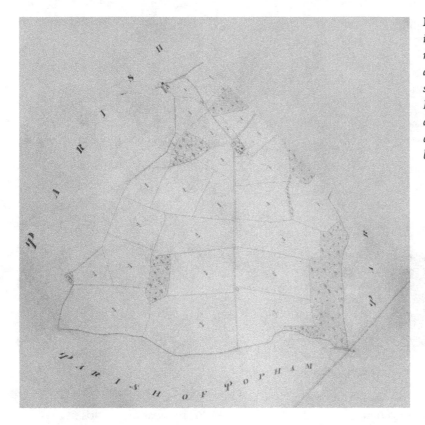

Map 4 *South Steventon in 1840 showing rectangular fields and lane running south from Warren Farm, with the church and manor house depicted on the eastern boundary of the parish.*

from the village that lends the station its name. The latter was opened as 'Andover Road' by the L&SWR in 1840 on the London to Southampton line.[33]

Carriers, Buses and Post

In Jane Austen's time coaches ran on the main roads to the north and south of the parish. Coaches operated by J. Cooke and Co. carrying passengers and parcels ran six days a week from Deane Gate to Salisbury, Basingstoke and London.[34] In 2015 Deane Gate was served by regular buses to Basingstoke, Andover and Winchester. Coaches also ran on weekdays along the Winchester to London road, calling at the Wheatsheaf in North Waltham parish. By 1859, the post came through Micheldever railway station to the local postmaster at the village post office, which was located at Steventon Arch.[35] Deliveries and collections were twice daily by 1875.[36] By 1898 mail deliveries and collections were

33   R.V.J. Butt, *The Directory of Railway Stations: details every public and private passenger station, halt, platform and stopping place, past and present* (Sparkford, 1995), 158, 179.
34   Austen, *Letters*, 36, 149 and 394, n. 1; HRO, 44M69/G1/187d, c (i).
35   *White's Dir.* (1859), 514; *Kelly's Post Office Dir.* (1867), 672.
36   *Post Office Dir. Hants.* (1875), 224.

Figure 4 *Tunnel under the railway embankment in 2014.*

routed through Whitchurch and by 1923 via Basingstoke.[37] The post office closed in 1978.[38] From 1930 to 1939 the village had one haulage contractor.[39]

Settlement, Population and Domestic Buildings

Early Settlement

Archaeological evidence shows the presence of human activity in the area from many different periods. The earliest evidence of human activity is a retouched flake of flint of Lower Palaeolithic date[40] from a site at the northern part of the parish on Cheesedown farm. There are more traces of the Bronze Age with two or three barrows in the south-west corner of the parish, adjacent to the scheduled group known as the Popham Beacons, which are just over the parish boundary in Overton[41] with two linear ditches[42] possibly associated with them. There is another small barrow[43] in Misholt Copse and several ring ditches (which probably represent ploughed-out barrows) are visible on

37   *Kelly's Dir. Hants.* (1898), 520; (1923), 639.
38   Tanner, *Steventon*, 14.
39   *Kelly's Dir. Winchester* (1930), 274; *Hants.* (1939), 540.
40   Hants. HER 59203.
41   Ibid., 18380, 18381.
42   Ibid., 38471.
43   Ibid., 18677.

Figure 5 *Fragment of cross shaft, believed to be 9th century, suggesting an early Christian presence.*

aerial photographs at Ashe Grove Copse[44] and west of Round Wood,[45] again with rectilinear ditches nearby.

Farmland in Steventon is rich in cropmarks visible on aerial photographs which represent early settlements and field systems and Ashe Park still has some visible lynchets.[46] The complex of cropmarks at Nurshanger farm[47] has been dated by metal detector finds to the Iron Age and Roman periods, as has the complex west of Misholt Copse.[48] Field walking has yielded pottery and coins at a site near Keepers Cottage[49] and at Cocksford Down.[50] Fragments of Roman pottery, including some Samian ware, were found in the garden of the old school house.

The early Anglo-Saxon core of the village probably lay on the chalk hilltop in the area of the later church and manor house. The church and manor house seem to have been present from at least the late 12th or early 13th century.[51] At some point settlement moved from the bare downland top to the valley below, where, although there was an absence of any continuous surface water, people would have found it easier to extract water from wells.

44 Hants. HER 38000.
45 Ibid., 38014, 38015.
46 Ibid., 18664.
47 Ibid., 38016.
48 Ibid., 54882.
49 Ibid., 50280.
50 Ibid., 38448.
51 See pp. 29, 89.

Figure 6 *St Nicholas Church.*

Settlement from 1700 to 2015

By 1700 there were three main areas of settlement: the original manorial/ecclesiastical centre; the village street to the south of the Triangle; and the area around the old rectory to the east of the Triangle along the lane to North Waltham, all in the northern half of the parish. In addition, there was some development at Deane Gate in the far north of the parish (Maps 5, 10 and 12). In the early 19th century the remaining settlement around the old rectory was pulled down and, from the mid 19th century, settlement extended from the Triangle north to the railway embankment beside the lane to Deane Gate in the area known as Steventon Arch (Map 7).

In 1741 the manor house stood next to the church on the hill at the eastern edge of the parish but the rectory (Fig. 24) was situated in the valley bottom, at the junction of the lane running downhill from the church (Maps 5, 13 and Fig. 7) and the lane from the Triangle to North Waltham. Between the rectory and the Triangle was the greatest concentration of housing with nine houses profiting from access to wells in the damp valley bottom (Map 5).[52]

These houses gradually disappeared between 1741 and 1840. There are various theories to account for this, ranging from flooding to dilapidations, the latter occurring

52   Randell's map of the farms from which the extract is taken is at HRO, 39M89/E/B/384.

Figure 7 *Lane from St Nicholas Church to the valley bottom and the site of the old rectory of Revd George Austen in 2014.*

Figure 8 *The Triangle in 2014 looking north towards Steventon Arch with Elmtree Cottages on the left and Quintans on the right.*

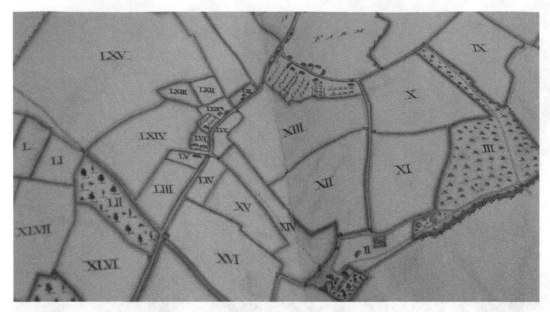

Map 5 *Main areas of settlement in 1741, extending south and east from the Triangle.*

Map 6 *Extract from the Steventon tithe map of 1839, showing Street Farm (plot number 62) as the only building in the valley bottom.*

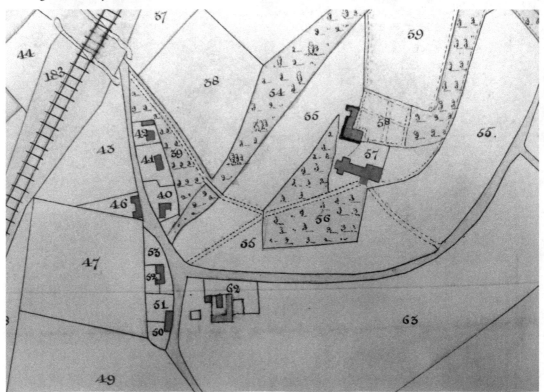

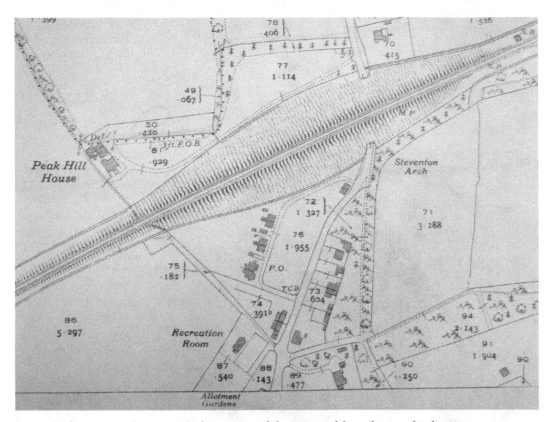

Map 7 *Settlement near Steventon Arch in 1942 and the impact of the railway embankment.*

as a result of the costly challenge Edward Knight faced from Mr and Miss Hinton to his inheritance of Thomas Knight's estate. [53]

The final three cottages on this lane and the old rectory survived in 1821 (Map 13).[54] The area was then transformed as Edward Knight commissioned a new rectory, later named Steventon House, for his son, William, on the hillside facing the old rectory.[55] He surrounded it with 50 a. of new glebe land which became a park. Both developments were designed to enhance the living and status of his son, William, whom he had recently appointed as rector of Steventon. The old rectory and the three remaining cottages were then demolished (*c.*1824), possibly as they did not enhance the view from the new gentleman's residence.

New farm buildings were constructed for Street Farm, the only building left in the valley bottom, which was leased to the rector and from which the new glebe was managed, on the south side of this lane where it joined the Triangle (Map 6).[56] In 2014 a modern dwelling, Patience House, occupied this site. Following the sale of the rectory

53   See p. 27.
54   HRO, 115A08/148/1.
55   See p. 77.
56   HRO, 79M78/B212.

Map 8 *Purchase by Elizabeth Knight of Dr Nicholls's freehold, 1736.*

A 2 barns, stable, carthouse, fodderhouse, orchard of 3/4 a. in decay and meadow of 3/4 a.

B a close above the meade of about $2^{1}/_{2}$ a.

G Barn close (2 a.)

K field next to Haseldown coppice (*c.*7 a.)

L the field next to K (*c.*7 a.)

M the field next to L (9 a.)

KLM are Cockley lands

Total of inclosed land 28.25 a.

Common field land:
Millway field (**P**) 12.5 a.
Middle field (**O**) 3 a.
Yonder field (**N**) 8.5 a.
0.5 a. in Bassetts close

in 1931, the village hall (Fig. 20) was built on the Triangle and Quintans (Fig. 8), a substantial house, was built on the hill overlooking the Triangle. In the late 20th century the far eastern end of the lane to North Waltham, farm buildings and an industrial estate were developed.

To the south of the Triangle, the modern village street developed steadily between 1741 and 2015, close to the dried-out valley which ran north from Warren Farm (Map 2). This replaced the area of settlement around the old rectory in the early 19th century. In 1741 five houses lay on the west side of the village street, with the most southerly being the farmhouse of New or Bassetts Farm (Map 5). Elmtree Cottages bordered the Triangle in the 18th century. As the cottages near the old rectory disappeared, more settlement developed around the Triangle and along the west side of this village street. The east

Figure 9 *Deane Gate Cottage in 2014.*

side of this street, by contrast, is arable farm land. Throughout the 19th century there is evidence of pulling down and rebuilding village cottages with most of the building being on this street.[57] In 1806 two cottages were built immediately west of the Triangle.[58] These were combined into one property, called Jasmine Cottage in 2015.[59] Further along the Street in the late 19th century Henry Harris built two sets of semi-detached cottages for estate workers or officials. Beyond these, in the 1890s the school and school mistress's houses were built. Just north-west of the school was the Methodist chapel built in 1903. Wheatley's Close, built in the 1950s, lay north of the school and chapel.[60]

A cottage was also built immediately east of Hatch Gate on Waltham Lane in 1737 but it appears to have been pulled down in 1845.[61] South of Hatch Gate, 19th-century development included Warren Farm and Warren Farm cottages. West of Warren Farm and isolated on the parish boundary was Litchfield Grange.[62] There were already a few houses north-west of the Triangle in 1741 but from the mid 19th century, a new area of settlement, known as Steventon Arch, developed between the Triangle and the railway embankment, just to the north of and along the road to Deane. Two pairs of red-brick semi-detached railway cottages were built by the L&SWR (1871–81) for signalmen, platelayers and their families in Stonehills, a very narrow lane on the side of the embankment north of, and parallel to, the lane to Deane.[63] Some in-filling has since taken place here. Opposite the railway cottages, on the lane to Deane, a number

57   HRO, 79M78/B211, B212, B213.
58   Ibid., 18M61/box K/bundle 5.
59   Basingstoke and Deane Conservation Area Appraisal: Steventon, 2004.
60   OS Map 1:2500, Hants. XXV.4 (1910 edn); Tanner, *Steventon*, 23.
61   HRO, 18M61/tin box C; 79M78/B212.
62   See pp. 32–3.
63   Census 1871, 1881; Tanner, *Steventon*, 15.

Figure 10 *Cottages at Bassetts Farm. Originally this was one farmhouse of c.1700 and is one of the oldest domestic buildings surviving in Steventon.*

Figure 11 *Pond Cottages with red-brick dressing surrounding flint work. This style dates from the lordship of Henry Harris and is noted in the conservation area appraisal.*

Figure 12 *Jasmine Cottage in 2015.*

Figure 13 *Elmtree Cottages on the Triangle in 2014.*

of cottages, including a smithy, were constructed.[64] By 1941 Steventon Arch had been
further developed and included a short-lived recreation room (Map 7), but the area, even
in 2015, retained a very rural atmosphere with many trees between the houses.

In the final area of development at Deane Gate, about one mile north of the village,
houses in the far north of the parish along the Andover to Basingstoke Road existed in
1741. Deane Gate comprised of an inn on the Andover to Basingstoke road with a few
cottages and shops at the northern end of the lane leading south towards Steventon Arch
(Map 1). Cheesedown Farm lay just south of Deane Gate and in 2014 its barns had been
converted into dwellings. By 1881 the brick built and slated house called the Firs, later
Peak Hill House, was built immediately north-west of the railway arch.[65]

Domestic Buildings

Few domestic buildings survive from before the 19th century. The old farmhouse on
Bassetts Farm, now divided into two cottages (Fig. 9), at the southern end of the village
street, is one of the oldest surviving dwellings and dates from the late 17th century or
early 18th century (Fig. 10).[66]

At the Triangle, the semi-detached Elm Cottages (Fig. 13) are well-preserved
examples of Hampshire vernacular cottages with distinctive outshots at either end. They
took their name from the Elm which used to grow on the Triangle. The cottages date
to the early 18th century, and 1738 has been suggested.[67] They appear on the 1741 map
(Map 5) but have been much modernized since.[68] They were built of brick and flint, with
structural brickwork around the jams and quoins. The roof slope is long and continuous
broken only by two chimney stacks. This and the line of the hip slopes indicates that they
were originally thatched. Jasmine Cottage (built 1806) nearby is also of brick and flint
construction (Fig. 12).

Most of the vernacular buildings of Steventon are of a relatively late date. In 2015,
the village was in a conservation area which reflects the importance of the two sets of
imposing and substantial semi-detached cottages from the late 19th century along the
main street between Wheatley's Close and the Old School built by Henry Harris and let
to tenants of the estate. These share the decorative use of red-brick dressing to embellish
coursed flint work (Fig. 11). The cottages have slated roofs.[69] Red-brick dressing was
also employed to decorate the Old School and Old School House (1894–5), where it
surrounds grey brick (Fig. 21).

The main farmhouse at Bassetts Farm was built in red brick in c.1880 by Henry
Harris.[70] The village hall (Fig. 20), built in 1932 in a simple arts and crafts design, on the
Triangle, fitted well with the vernacular style of the settlement.[71]

---

64   OS Map 1:2500, Hants. XXV.4 (1872 edn).
65   HRO, 46M84/F86/2.
66   It has proved impossible to gain access to determine this.
67   Pers. comm. from Geoff Mann, 3 July 2014: a brick bearing that date was discovered by the householder
      of no. 1 Elmtree Cottages.
68   Basingstoke and Deane, Steventon Conservation Area Report 2004; HRO, 39M89/E/B/384.
69   Basingstoke and Deane Conservation Area Report 2004, http://www.basingstoke.gov.uk/NR/rdonlyres/
      DC293686-2940-40DF-801F-0E1042CA0674/0/Steventon.pdf (accessed 10 April 2013).
70   HRO, 71M82/PZ5.
71   See p. 66.

Population

Until the 18th century Steventon was a very small village with between 16 and 18 houses, all situated in the north of the parish. In 1086 Domesday Book listed five villeins, three bordars and eight slaves.[72] In 1327 seven landholders were assessed to pay a total of 9*s.* 8*d.* in the Hampshire lay subsidy.[73] In 1524–5 there were 18 taxpayers.[74] There is a suggestion of epidemic disease, perhaps plague, with the deaths of four people who were related in July and August 1533.[75] There were 40 communicants in 1603[76] and 53 in 1676, indicating a rising population.[77] Sixteen houses were listed in the hearth tax in 1665, suggesting a population of 72–80.[78] In 1725, according to the rector, the population was about 80 but increasing as births averaged three to four a year and burials one to two.[79] Some cottages and Warren Farm were built in the 18th and early 19th centuries as the population, following the national trend, rose to 153 in 1801. In the first two decades of the 19th century the population remained almost static: there were 151 residents in 1821. The following decade saw a dramatic increase and in 1831 there were 197 people living in 32 houses as new houses were built along the main village street.[80] This expansion continued. By 1851 there were 187 inhabitants in 37 houses, falling to 167 in 1861 before resuming the upward trend. There were 199 residents in 1871 and 288, living in 59 dwellings, in 1881. In 1881 some of the increase was due to craftsmen lodging in the village while building a new mansion house for Henry Harris, the new landlord. The population then fell to 239 in 1891 and 229 in 56 houses in 1901, before rising to 250 in 57 houses in 1911.[81] Thereafter there was a noticeable decline to 195 in 50 houses in 1921, when a number of cottages were empty.[82] The population recovered to 233 in 57 houses in 1931[83] and has stayed fairly constant in the 20th century, although most of them lived in smaller households. There were 219 inhabitants living in 85 houses in 2001 and 207 in 2011 in 81 houses.[84]

72   *Domesday,* 124.
73   TNA, E 179/173/4.
74   J. Sheail, ed. R.W. Hoyle, 'The regional distribution of wealth in England as indicated in the 1524/5 Lay Subsidy returns', *List and Index Society,* Special Series, 29 (1998), II, 199.
75   HRO, 1533B/40, 1533B/38, 1533B/31, 1535B/34. The last reference, a will, has been catalogued as 1535 but was in fact proved in 1533.
76   *Dioc. Pop. Rtns,* 490.
77   *Compton Census,* 85. The question was slightly different in 1676 asking how many in the parish were of an age to take communion.
78   *Hearth Tax,* 239.
79   *Parson and Parish,* 127.
80   HRO, 79M78/B211–12.
81   Census 1801–1911.
82   HRO, 23M71/LB1, 364–5.
83   *Warren's District Dir.* (1939) 368.
84   Census 1851–1901. Basingstoke and Deane, http://www.basingstoke.gov.uk (accessed 4 June 2013); census 2001, 2011.

MANORS AND OTHER ESTATES

DOMESDAY BOOK RECORDED THAT a single estate existed in Steventon in 1066.[1] Later, the rectorial glebe existed as a separate entity, but by 1611 it had been permanently added to the manorial estate.[2] From the 16th century, and probably long before that, there was also part of a freehold estate in the south-west of the parish, 127 a. in 1839, which belonged to South Litchfield Grange in the neighbouring parish of Ashe.[3]

Steventon Manor

Ælfhelm held the manor in 1066 and Alsige *berchenistre* (the porter?), a king's thegn, held it in 1086.[4] In the 12th century, Steventon came into the hands of the de Luverez family as can be seen in its grants of land to the church.[5] A Geoffrey de Luverez granted land in Steventon to Waverley Abbey *c.*1147[6] and Michael de Luverez was lord of the manor by 1190;[7] he held a half knight's fee in 1194–5, and in 1202–13.[8] But the fall of Normandy to the French in 1204 posed a dilemma for many such landowners who held land in both England and France, and whose dual loyalties had been reflected in the grant of English land to a French monastery, albeit to one with an English subsidiary. Michael chose to stay in his French lands and therefore forfeited his rights to his English possessions, which would technically escheat to the crown. His brother, Geoffrey, one of the bishop of Winchester's household knights from at least 1210–11, and de facto his household steward, sought to retain Steventon and paid a fine of 50 marks to King John for possession of the manor.[9] In 1231 Geoffrey was summoned by Henry III to show by what right he held the manor, which was alleged to have escheated or forfeited to the king.[10] In 1233 Henry III either dismissed the Luverez claim, or it lapsed on the death of Geoffrey, and the king now granted the land in Steventon, which had belonged to

1   This is contrary to the view expressed in *VCH Hants*. IV, 171, that a second estate, held by Godwine the Falconer (*Domesday*, 124), existed in the 11th century and coalesced by 1167, but the evidence does not back up the assertion made there.
2   TNA, STAC 8/811.
3   HRO, 21M65/F71/223/1 and 2; 39M89/E/B/384.
4   *Domesday*, 124. Alsige also held Enham (Knights Enham, later Enham Alamein) in 1086, ibid.123.
5   *See* Vincent, *Acta*, 206–7, 212–5.
6   O. Manning and W. Bray, *The History and Antiquities of the County of Surrey*, III (1814, repr. 1974), 145–6. The deeds are undated. 1147 comes from the bull of Pope Eugenius III which records Waverley's land and rights.
7   Bodleian Library, MS DD Queen's 241.
8   *The Red Book of the Exchequer*, 91, 148.
9   *Pipe Roll* 13 Hen. II (1166–7) (PRS, 1889), 190.
10 *Cal. Close*, 1227–1231, 581, Vincent, *Acta: IX, Winchester* 1205–38, 207.

Geoffrey de Luverez, to Geoffrey des Roches, nephew of Peter des Roches, the bishop of Winchester.[11] In addition to his national importance, Peter dominated government at a county level and would have been important in securing for Geoffrey both a Hampshire heiress and Steventon itself.[12] In 1234, Geoffrey des Roches held the manor at royal pleasure.[13] Following Peter des Roches's fall from favour and banishment from the king's court in April 1234, the des Roches tenure of Steventon was challenged by the heirs of Geoffrey de Luverez. His sister, Annora, wife of Hugh de Wengham, and his nephew, Philip de Sandervill, together paid the king a fine of £80 to recover possession of the manor.[14]

In 1236 a Nicholas de Luverez was involved in a dispute over land in Steventon.[15] In 1249 Steventon was held jointly by Manser de Sandervill, probably son and heir of Philip de Sandervill, and Hugh de Wengham, the son and successor of Hugh and Annora.[16] In 1250 Hugh de Wengham stated that after his death his son, Geoffrey, would inherit his property in Long Sutton (Hants.)[17] and Steventon and that in the meantime he would provide food and clothing for his son and daughter-in-law, Egelina, and their children.[18] Nevertheless, the des Roches family regained Steventon. Firstly, Martin des Roches, son of Geoffrey, purchased the half owned by Geoffrey and Egelina c.1251–60 and then apparently purchased the half of Manser de Sandervill.[19] In 1258, a Michael Luverez quitclaimed his rights in Steventon to Martin.[20] Thus in 1275 Martin des Roches held land assessed at 2½ hides in Steventon in return for 40 days military service.[21] Martin (d. 1277) left to his brother, Hugh, in Steventon manor, a messuage and two carucates of arable land and 100 a. of land, worth 23s. a year, held of John de Maneriis, for which the service was not specified, containing in total 360 a., each acre being worth 4d. a year. He also possessed £5 in free rents and £3 12s. in villein rents and labour services worth £2 10s. and 300 sheep on a common pasture; the total value was about £20.[22] John des Roches (d. 1288) similarly held Steventon for the king for 40 days a year serving in Wales.[23] He left the manor to his son, John, aged 22 in 1288, and his heirs.[24] In 1336 John de Roches settled the manor and the advowson of the church on himself, his wife, Joan, and their heirs.[25] John predeceased his wife, who died in 1361. Joan was succeeded by her and John's daughter, Mary, widow of John de Boarhunt. Mary married a second husband,

11   *Cal. Close*, 1231–4, 282; on Geoffrey des Roches see Vincent, *Acta: IX,* 212–5; *Cal Pat.*, 1232–47, 38.
12   *ODNB*, s.v. 'Roches, Peter des (d. 1238)', accessed 25 Nov. 2014; N. Vincent, *Peter des Roches: an alien in English politics 1205–1238*, (Cambridge, 1996), 184–95; 359–60; Vincent, *Acta*, 213.
13   *Cal Pat.* 1232–47, 38 (indexed as Steventon, co. Beds but clearly Hants.).
14   *Excerpta e Rot. Fin.* I, 261; TNA C 60/33 m. 5.
15   Vincent, *Acta*, 207.
16   TNA, CP 25/1/203/8/64.
17   *VCH Hants.* IV, 19.
18   TNA, CP 25/1/204/9/5.
19   Ibid., CP 25/1/204/10/31.
20   Vincent, *Acta*, 207.
21   *Rot. Hund.* II, i, 221.
22   *Cal. Inq. p.m.* XI, p. 136; Burrows, *Brocas*, 332–4.
23   Ibid., V, p. 175.
24   TNA, C 143/92/3.
25   Ibid., C 143/233/2.

Sir Bernard Brocas (d. 1398) of Beaurepaire, Sherborne St John, near Basingstoke.[26] This was the start of a long connection between Beaurepaire and Steventon which continued into the 17th century. Sir Bernard Brocas, of Gascon descent, was a soldier, knighted in 1354, made a knight of Edward III's chamber in 1361.[27] He was captain of Calais castle in the 1370s and after the death of Edward III, Brocas served his grandson, Richard II. In recognition of his services, Bernard was buried in St Edmund's chapel in Westminster Abbey.[28] He was succeeded by his son, also Sir Bernard, who was executed in early 1400 for his involvement in the Epiphany Rising against Henry IV.[29] His son, William (1379–1456), was allowed to inherit Beaurepaire and Steventon.[30] William was master of the king's buckhounds, a Hampshire MP from 1414 to 1422 and three times sheriff of Hampshire. He married secondly (by June 1414) Joan, daughter of Sir William Sandys, and added Sherborne Cowdray, later known as the Vyne, to his properties.[31] On William's death (1456), he was succeeded by his elder son, also William (d. 1484). This William was succeeded by his son, John (d. 1484) and grandson, John (d. 1492), who in turn was succeeded by his son, William (d. 1506), whose heirs were his two daughters, Anne and Edith.[32] Edith became the sole heir on the death of her sister and married Sir Ralph Pexall, who succeeded her at Beaurepaire and Steventon from 1517 to c.1537.[33] Sir Richard Pexall, son of Edith and Ralph, and master of the king's buckhounds, succeeded his father and was rebuilding Steventon manor house as a Tudor mansion, from c.1560 to his death in 1571, at which time one wing was constructed.[34] Sir Richard Pexall also attempted (c.1538) to increase his demesne by inclosing and sowing with corn 300 a. of common on Southdown[35] on which the rector and people of the parish had pasture rights. Pexall was ordered to take down his fences and restore the common.[36] Sir Richard was buried near Sir Bernard Brocas in the St Edmund Chapel of Westminster Abbey.[37] Problems over his will (1571) seriously affected the descent of the manor of Steventon.[38] Sir Richard had four daughters with his first wife but after her death he had married Elinor Cotgrave, to whom he left his estates for 13 years until his grandson, Sir Pexall Brocas, son of his eldest daughter, Ann, and Sir Bernard Brocas of Horton, came of age.[39] Elinor was his executrix, charged to pay dowries of £500 each to his three younger daughters, Margery Beckett, Elizabeth Jobson and Barbara Bridges, but the will was judged to be unlawful as Sir Richard should have left at least one third of his estate to his legal heirs, his four daughters. Bequests of one third of Pexall's land in Beaurepaire and Steventon were declared invalid and this third was divided between his four

26   *Cal. Inq. p.m.*, XI, p. 166; TNA, C 143/233/2, 338/12.
27   *ODNB*, s.v. 'Brocas, Sir Bernard (*c*.1330–95), soldier and administrator' (accessed 13 Nov. 2014).
28   Ibid.; *Hist. Parl. Commons*, 1386–1421, ii, 359–62.
29   Burrows, *Brocas*, 136; *ODNB*, s.v. 'Brocas, Sir Bernard'.
30   *Hist. Parl. Commons*, 1386–1421 ii, 363–4; *Feudal Aids*, III, 344, 364.
31   *Hist. Parl. Commons*, 1386–1421, ii, 363–4.
32   Burrows, *Brocas*, 165–71.
33   *VCH Hants.* IV, 165–6.
34   Burrows, *Brocas*, 333; HRO, 46M74/PZ91.
35   The location of Southdown is not known except that it must have been south of the village streets.
36   TNA, C 78/3/98.
37   Burrows, *Brocas*, 201.
38   HRO, 46M74/PZ91.
39   Burrows, *Brocas*, 208.

daughters and their husbands, giving each couple one twelfth of the whole estate. Two of the twelfths were acquired by Sir Bernard and Ann Brocas of Horton: one as Ann's inheritance and the other purchased, 1572–3, from Ann's sister, Barbara Bridges. Both of these were inherited in 1591 by Sir Pexall Brocas giving him ten twelfths of the estates of Beaurepaire and Steventon.[40] Two of these twelfths remained independent of the Beaurepaire estate until 1633 when Sir Thomas Brocas purchased them.[41] Elizabeth was married to John Jobson of Essex and together they sold their twelfth to Dame Elinor and her second husband, Sir John Savage.[42] This one twelfth was inherited by Sir John Savage's second son, Edward Savage, who was outlawed for debt in 1615 and died 1622 leaving all to his son, who held it until 1633.[43] The share of John Beckett, which was purchased by Richard Walter, also descended separately from the main estate until 1633.[44]

Dame Elinor and Sir John Savage refused to give up Beaurepaire when Sir Pexall Brocas came of age in 1584 and tried to settle Beaurepaire on their son, Edward Savage, to the extent that a map of Beaurepaire in 1613 was drawn up for the worshipful Edward Savage.[45] Lady Elinor (d. 1618) had two more husbands after the death of Sir John Savage.

Sir Pexall Brocas, deprived of Beaurepaire, lived at Steventon from 1584, which he had also inherited through his mother. He was master of the king's buckhounds from 1584.[46] Brocas was also MP for Steyning (Sussex) from 1584 with Thomas Shirley II, his brother-in-law, who encouraged Brocas to rebel with the earl of Essex in February 1601.[47] Brocas was pardoned in 1604 for his part in the rebellion.[48] In 1592 Pexall Brocas with his father-in-law, Thomas Shirley of Wiston (Sussex) in the name of himself and his wife, Margaret, had settled their ten-twelfths of Steventon on themselves and then on their son, Thomas (b. 1591).[49] Sir Pexall Brocas, according to allegations made against him in the Court of Star Chamber in 1605,[50] was an unscrupulous lord of the manor, who alienated his son, his rectors and his tenants.[51] Sir Pexall Brocas was resident in Steventon in December 1611, when the death of his servant, Agnes, was recorded.[52] In the same year he tried to use a fine to bar the entail and sell his rights in Steventon to Edmund Brockett and others. This was to be achieved by a device involving a lease for ever of 4 a. of Steventon, known as Pigeon House to John Beckett, for which Beckett was to levy a fine in the Court of Common Pleas.[53] Sir Pexall's son, Thomas, reacted by invading Steventon and driving his father and his household out of Steventon manor house by force. Thomas seized the manor from his father's servants, supported by manorial tenants and freeholders, including John Crook who wore coats of mail and were armed with 'swords, daggers,

40   Burrows, *Brocas*, 210.
41   Ibid., 228–9.
42   TNA, C 2/JasI/M8/15; Burrows, *Brocas*, 210, 213.
43   TNA, E 178/4510; *Hist. Parl. Commons*, 1604–1629 vi, 217.
44   TNA, C 2/JasI/M8/15.
45   Burrows, *Brocas*, 211–13.
46   *Cal. SP Dom.*, 1603–10, 24, 211.
47   *Hist. Parl. Commons*, 1558–1603 ii, 485–6.
48   *Cal. SP Dom.*, 1603–10, 69.
49   Shirley was either Brocas's father-in-law or his brother-in-law: HRO, 18M61/box E/bundle 9.
50   TNA, STAC 8/8/11.
51   See Social, Economic and Religious History below.
52   HRO, 71M82/PR1. Agnes was buried on 3 December 1611.
53   HRO, 18M61/box E/bundle 9; TNA, E 214/1028, 1357.

long picks, staves, forest bills, bowes and arrows, guns, pistols & other weapons'.[54] Thomas and his supporters broke down the doors of the mansion house and broke into chests and coffers to steal all the documents relating to his father's rights in the land. Thomas and his wife Elizabeth then occupied this house containing agricultural and household goods worth £3,000.[55] Sir Pexall then alleged that his son, Thomas, had tried to have him murdered firstly by stabbing and secondly by bribing servants to poison him.[56] Sir Pexall had been summoned by the Privy Council, the Court of Requests and Star Chamber but refused to attend to account for his actions and finally he was excommunicated for 'his reversions and adulteries' by the archbishop of Canterbury on 10 June 1613.[57] He paid large fines to be pardoned for his offences.[58] In 1611 Sir Pexall Brocas moved to Little Brickhill (Bucks.) which he had inherited through his father, living there or in London until his death in 1630. He renounced all rights to Steventon to his son.[59] In his will, Sir Pexall charged his son, Thomas, to pay all his debts out of his manors and lands. No mention was made of Steventon, which by that time had been sold by his son.[60]

Sir Thomas Brocas continued to live at Steventon, where his three children were born between 1615 and 1619.[61] In 1622 he mortgaged Steventon to Sir Thomas Jervoise of Herriard and Sir Henry Browne of Writtle (Essex). In 1626 Sir Thomas Brocas regained his main family manor of Beaurepaire and ceased to live in Steventon. In 1625 Brocas sold his ten-twelfths of the manor and advowson of the church for £5,300 to Sir Thomas Coteel the Younger,[62] a moneylender and trader of London, who converted much of his and his father, Sir Thomas Coteel the elder's, assets into land.[63] Steventon served as Coteel's family seat from 1625–33. In 1628 Coteel also purchased Litchfield in the adjoining parish of Ashe with some land in Steventon.[64] In 1633 he sold his ten-twelfths of the manor of Steventon and the rectory for £5,000 to Thomas Brocas, and then lived at his adjoining estate of Litchfield, Ashe.[65] Brocas was still in financial difficulties, having purchased the two independent twelfths of Steventon in 1633 and having been charged to pay all his father's debts in 1630, so in 1635 he mortgaged Steventon to Sir John Baker and Richard Parkhurst, trustees to George Mynne (I), lord of the manor of Epsom (Surrey).[66] For the next 250 years the lords of the manor were non-resident. Mynne died in 1648 and in 1649 his widow, Anne, purchased Steventon and left it to her son, also George.[67] George Mynne (II) died childless in 1651 leaving the manor to

54   TNA, STAC 8/82/3.
55   Ibid.
56   Ibid.
57   Ibid., STAC 8/8/11; 8/82/3; *Acts of PC* (1591–2), 488–9.
58   HRO, 44M69/F2/14/47/1–3.
59   *Hist. Parl. Commons*, 1558–1603, ii, 485–6; *VCH Bucks*. IV, 300.
60   TNA, PROB 11/158/333.
61   HRO, 71M82/PR1.
62   Ibid., 18M61/box E/bundle 9. *VCH Hants*. IV, 172, states that it was not clear whether Thomas Coteel the elder or the younger purchased Steventon. The sale document from Coteel to Brocas 1633 was signed by the purchaser, Thomas Coteel the Younger.
63   HRO, 18M61/box E/bundle 9.
64   *Hist. Parl. Commons*, 1604–29, iii, 686–89.
65   HRO, 18M61/box E/bundle 9; *Hist. Parl. Commons*, 1604–29, iii, 686–89.
66   *Hist. Parl. Commons*, 1604–29, v, 471–3; HRO, 18M61/box E/bundle 9.
67   HRO, 18M61/box E/bundle 9.

his sisters: Anne, who married first Sir John Lewknor of West Dean, north of Chichester in West Sussex, and secondly Sir William Morley of Halnaker (Sussex) and Elizabeth, who married Richard Evelyn of Woodcote, Epsom, younger brother of the author, John Evelyn. The Lewknors kept Steventon Manor House as a secondary residence and, initially with the Evelyns, held courts there until 1700.[68] Anne inherited all the estate when her sister died childless in 1692 and she was succeeded in 1704 by her son, John Lewknor (d. 1707), MP for Midhurst (Sussex).[69] Lewknor bequeathed the estate to William Knight, born William Woodward, husband of his cousin, Elizabeth, and MP for Midhurst from 1713 to 1721.[70] Elizabeth had changed her name from Martin to Knight to inherit the Knight estate at Chawton (Hants.) in 1702.[71] William died in 1721 and in 1725 Elizabeth married Bulstrode Peachey who also assumed the name of Knight.[72] Elizabeth bequeathed the estate to her cousin, Thomas May, a landowner in Godmersham (Kent) who was born Thomas Brodnax, but had already changed his name to May in 1727 to inherit a fortune from Sir Thomas May. May changed his name to Knight in 1738 to inherit Elizabeth's estate.[73] Thomas Knight married Jane Monck, whose second cousin was the Revd George Austen, Jane Austen's father, whom Knight appointed as rector of Steventon in 1761.[74] Knight owned Steventon manor until his death in 1781, when he was succeeded by his son, Thomas, who had married Catherine Knatchbull in 1779.[75] Thomas and Catherine Knight visited Steventon and were very impressed by Edward, third son of the Revd George Austen and brother of Jane. Their marriage proved to be childless so they adopted Edward Austen, and made him their heir. Edward Austen married Elizabeth, daughter of Sir Brook Bridges, in 1792 and lived at Rowling near Goodnestone (Kent) until the death of Thomas Knight in 1797 when he moved into Godmersham, whilst Catherine Knight drew an annuity of £2,000 from the estate and retired to White Friars House in Canterbury.[76] Edward Austen changed his name to Knight, following the death of Catherine in November 1812.[77]

Edward Knight faced a costly challenge to his lordship of Steventon and Chawton in 1814 from Mr and Miss Hinton, supported by James Baverstoke, on the grounds that Elizabeth Knight's will, 1738, had left her estate to the Hintons if Thomas Brodnax/May's line failed.[78] Thomas Knight, father and son, had broken the entail but the Hintons tried to prove an error in the process, serving a writ of ejectment on Edward in October 1815. The lawsuit was not settled until April 1818 when Edward was obliged to pay £15,000 to buy out the interest of his opponents.[79] Edward Knight developed Chawton House as his main residence in Hampshire. In 1852 he was succeeded by his son, Edward, who in 1855 sold his Steventon lands (Manor farm (1076 a.), Cheesedown farm (201 a.) and Warren

68   HRO, 18M61/box C/bundle 4; box E/bundle 9.
69   *Hist. Parl. Commons*, 1690–1715, 635–6.
70   HRO, 18M61/box G/bundle 10; *Hist. Parl. Commons*, 1690–1715, 579–80.
71   Grover, *Hyde*, 50.
72   Ibid., 51.
73   Austen, *Letters*, 541.
74   *Family Record*, 6.
75   TNA, PROB 11/1076/160.
76   Austen, *Letters*, 356, n. 2 to L. 4; 17.
77   Ibid., 408, n. 5.
78   Grover, *Hyde,* 58.
79   *Family Record,* 195.

farm (490 a.)), to the second duke of Wellington for £41,939 13*s.* 8*d.*, to raise money to complete the purchase of the Godmersham church estates.[80] The lordship of the manor and the advowson, rectory, glebe and rented land in Street farm were exempted out of the sale at the request of Edward's brother, the rector, William Knight. It is very probable that William wished to buy them himself but he and his brother were unable to agree terms. The lordship of the manor and the rectory were sold separately to the Revd Gilbert Alder in *c.*1860.[81] The duke of Wellington sold his Steventon estate in 1877 to Henry Harris, a wealthy corn factor from nearby Longparish.[82]

Harris's purchase inaugurated a new phase in the village's development. Much of the late 19th-century building activity in the village took place under Harris. He lived in the parish and replaced the old Elizabethan manor house with a new Victorian mansion (Fig. 14).[83] The lordship of the manor was reunited with its lands in 1901 when Harris purchased it from Naomi Alder, widow of Gilbert Alder's son, Revd Edward Alder, but Mrs Alder retained the advowson of the rectory.[84] In 1910 the manor, comprising the residence; a park of 170 a. with the old Tudor manor house still standing in the garden;[85] and 1,632 a. (let for 1,000 guineas a year, exclusive of the sporting rights) was sold to Robert H. D. Mills, who also purchased South Litchfield Grange.[86] In 1926 the estate was described as a fine residential estate with nearly 2,000 a. including 403 a. of woods and 28 a. of pleasure gardens. The increased acreage from 1910 was due to Robert Mills also possessing Litchfield Grange with its 306 a. stud farm, mainly in Ashe Parish but with some land in Steventon.[87]

Mr and Mrs Jack Onslow Fane purchased the estate in 1926.[88] Jack Onslow Fane was president of the British Boxing Board of Control from 1948 to 65.[89] The Manor House was destroyed by fire in 1932, after which the Onslow Fanes built a new house incorporating the old Tudor manor (Fig. 16). In 1936 they sold the manor to Captain and Mrs Bernard Hutton Croft.[90] The house was requisitioned by the London division of the National Fire Service as a training centre and base for a bomb disposal squad in 1940. The Hutton Crofts moved to the former rectory, Steventon House. The lords never again lived in the Manor House, which was leased by Hilsea College from 1947 to 1948.[91] Captain Hutton Croft died in 1961 and his widow, Vera Hutton Croft, in 1967.[92] Her executors sold the estate to Angus Mackinnon, whose family owned it until 1987, when it was sold to a wealthy house builder, Charles Church. Church restored and

80   HRO, 39M89/E/T26; 34A12/1; 79M78/B213–14.
81   Ibid., 39M89/E/B76.
82   MERL, Wellington/1622/34.
83   Ibid., Wellington/1622/34; *Post Office Dir.* (1875), 224; TNA, RG 11/1257.
84   HRO, 46M84/C27/2/1; *Kelly's Dir. Hants.* (1903), 548.
85   HRO, 62A00/1.
86   *VCH Hants.* IV, 198.
87   HRO, 46M84/F86/3.
88   *Kelly's Dir. Hants.* (1931), 614.
89   http://wbcboxing.com/wbceng/component/content/article/29-presidentes/1086-the-british-boxing-board-of-control (accessed 17 Jan. 2014).
90   *Kelly's Dir. Hants.* (1939), 540.
91   HRO, 51M76/P/5/51.
92   Tanner, *Steventon*, 5.

flew Supermarine Spitfire aircraft and was killed in 1989 when one of them crashed.[93] The estate was then partitioned and sold in freehold lots. In 2014 Steventon parish was divided into four freehold farms. To the north of the railway was Cheesedown (350 a.), which was farmed from Oakley; the farmhouse and building had been converted for domestic use;[94] and to the south was Stoken farm (300 a.), while Bassetts' 400 a. dairy farm lay in the centre of the parish, with Warren farm, which included lands of Litchfield Grange, extending to the southern boundary of the parish.

The Manor Houses

The history of the manor house can be divided into four main phases, with the core of the buildings on two adjacent sites.[95] A substantial early medieval stone house existed, in an area where stone would have had to be imported. Henry Harris, a later owner, commented in 1895 'I have preserved hundreds of tons of Norman worked stones which had been built into old walls and out of which I believe the Brocas manor is built'.[96] While the dating must be treated with caution, it suggests a large-scale early building, and the first edition of the *VCH Hants.* in 1911, produced when some of the stone was still visible, suggested a general date in the 12th and 13th century, and for a surviving large respond capital a date of *c.*1130.[97]

Joan des Roches had a capital messuage at Steventon on her death in 1361.[98] In the mid 16th century Richard Pexall began to rebuild the house. He built a new wing, which was unfinished at his death. In his will he trusted that his executrix, Elinor, his second wife, would finish his house at Steventon, but she clearly failed to do so.[99] Pexall's wing was a two-storey building, with two large projecting chimney stacks and at the end a projecting bay with large mullioned windows. Part of this building survived until the late 20th century, although much altered (Fig. 15).[100] The manor house was demolished in 1970.[101]

From 1633, Steventon ceased to be the lord's main residence, and by the later 17th century they had ceased to live there at all. Subsequently, the house was in the possession of the lessee of the estate, such as the Digweeds. It seems aptly described in White's directory as 'an old Elizabethan mansion finely mantled with ivy'.[102] It was only in 1877, when the manor was purchased by Henry Harris, who intended to live in Steventon, that a new house was built (1880–2).[103] This was built on a new but adjacent site with the old Pexall wing being gutted and converted into stables. The new house was designed by

93   'Charles Church', *The Times*, 3 July 1989.
94   *Southern Evening Echo*, 1 Apr. 1985.
95   The most recent treatment is in Pevsner, *North Hampshire*, 498.
96   H. Henshaw, *Steventon Hampshire, Historical notes and anecdotes* (1949 repr. 1997), unpag.
97   *VCH Hants.* IV, 173.
98   *Cal. Inq. p.m.*, XI, p. 166; TNA, C 143/233/2, 338/12.
99   HRO, 46M74/PZ91.
100 Ibid., 62A00/1.
101 Tanner, *Steventon*, 5.
102 *White's Dir. Hants. & IOW* (1859), 514.
103 There is disagreement on the precise dating. I have followed Pevsner, *North Hampshire*. The 1908 sale particulars give 1874 before Harris had acquired the manor. Work on the Pexall range seems to have been underway in 1877. D. Tweedle, M. Biddle and B.Kjφlbe-Biddle, *Corpus of Anglo-Saxon Stone Sculpture*, IV, *S.E. England* (1993), 267. See also the 1881 census.

Figure 14 *Manor House in 1908, designed by Alfred Waterhouse.*

the eminent Victorian architect, Alfred Waterhouse, who was recognised for his design
of public buildings such as the British Museum of Natural History in London, and
Manchester Town Hall, but who also built up a portfolio of country house building of
which Blackmoor House (1865–73), provided a nearby and recent example.[104] His design
for Harris at Steventon was in the Jacobethan style and was constructed in brick with
stone details (Fig. 14).[105] It was described in 1898 as a mansion of red brick and stone in
a well-wooded park of 170 a.[106] In 1908 the house was a large building, featuring modern
technology. There was an entrance hall, saloon, drawing room, library, billiard room,
business room and boudoir and day and night nurseries. There were 11 bedrooms for
family and guests, hot and cold water, drinking water pumped to a tank in the top of the
house and hot-air heating. The domestic accommodation, with its servants' hall, kitchen,
laundry, housekeeper's room and butler's pantry, was entirely shut off from the principle
rooms. Some of the stonework of the Elizabethan manor house was recycled and used for
the fernery and other garden features, and its shell converted into stables. The gardens
included terraces, lawns and flower parterres, a yew walk, camellia and fern houses and
a walled kitchen garden with glass houses. In addition to the stables, the further advance
of modernity was reflected by the addition of 'a timber and corrugated iron motor house'.
In 1926 the room arrangements of the Manor House remained similar. There was a
tennis lawn, formal gardens and a woodland park amounting to 20 a. in Steventon with a
further 7 a. in North Waltham.[107]

   A major fire in 1932 led to the demolition of most of the Waterhouse/Harris building.
The owner, Fane, replaced this with a new stone built house in the Elizabethan style

104   *ODNB*, s.v. 'Alfred Waterhouse, (1830–1905), architect' (accessed 1 Aug. 2014).
105   HRO, 62A00/1; 46M84/F86/3; 29M96/85.
106   *Kelly's Dir. Hants.* (1898), 520.
107   HRO, 46M84/F86/3.

Figure 15 *Tudor wing of Manor House, 1911.*

Figure 16 *Manor House c.1935, built in Elizabethan style after the fire of 1932.*

(1935). The remaining wing of the original Elizabethan house was retained and became one side wing of the new house (Fig. 16).[108]

The Manor House was requisitioned during the Second World War and continued to suffer neglect afterwards and was demolished in 1970,[109] serving as hard core for the M3 motorway, then under construction. A surviving part of the Waterhouse service buildings was then developed into a neo-Tudor replacement of *c.*1990,[110] and in 2014 this in turn was undergoing major extensions. Fragments of the 19th-century fernery also survive.[111]

Other Estates

Litchfield Grange

From the 12th century, two holdings grew up on the basis of land grants to monastic institutions. The most significant was Litchfield Grange which represented the lands acquired by Waverley abbey (Surrey). Litchfield Grange, centred in Ashe parish at a farmstead which straddled the parish boundary, included land in Steventon. By 1147, Geoffrey de Luverez granted a yardland in Steventon to the Cistercian house of Waverley

108 N. Pevsner and D. Lloyd, *The Buildings of England: Hampshire and the Isle of Wight* (1967), 611, describes this as the work of Morrison Marnock and of 1875–6, but this cannot be correct. This house postdates the brick Waterhouse buildings. This is not included in the new edition, *Pevsner, North Hampshire*, 499.
109 *Hampshire Chronicle*, 30 May 1970; Tanner, *Steventon*, 5.
110 Le Faye, *Steventon*, 16.
111 Site visit, 2014.

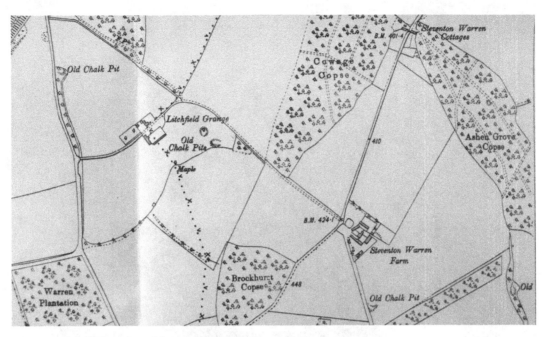

Map 9 *Litchfield Grange and Steventon Warren Farm, 1911.*

abbey,[112] and he was probably the Geoffrey who held the manor in 1166–7.[113] The grant to Waverley was subsequently confirmed by Adelza and then by Michael de Luverez.[114] Another grant to the same abbey at a nearby village was witnessed by Geoffrey de Luverez and Ingelrun de Luviers.[115] With other grants in nearby parishes, these were brought together to form Litchfield Grange which remained in the possession of Waverley until the Dissolution of the monasteries when it was granted to Sir William Fitzwilliam, who became earl of Southampton in 1537.[116] On his death it was inherited by his half-brother and then the latter's son, Anthony (created Viscount Montagu in 1554). In 1567, he sold the grange with 580 a. including freehold land in Steventon and land in Overton, Ashe and Quidhampton (Hants.) to Roger Hunt.[117] Sir Thomas Coteel the Younger purchased Litchfield in 1628 and left it to his nephew, Piers Edgcumbe, in 1640.[118] The grange was owned by the Edgcumbe family until the mid 18th century. In 1760 it was sold by Lord Edgcumbe to Mr Macreth.[119] It was sold frequently during the 19th century and in 1839 was owned by John Stevens, when the land in Steventon parish comprised 127 a.[120] Robert Mills had purchased Litchfield Grange and Steventon Manor by 1910, after which time Litchfield Grange descended with the main manor (Map 9).

112 Manning and Bray, *The History ... Surrey*, 145–6. The deeds are undated. 1147 comes from the bull of Pope Eugenius III which records Waverley's land and rights.
113 Pipe Roll 13 Hen II (Pipe Roll Society), 190.
114 Manning and Bray, *The History ... Surrey*, 145–6.
115 Ibid., 146.
116 *VCH Hants.* IV, 200.
117 Ibid.
118 *Hist. Parl. Commons*, 1604–29, iii, 686–89.
119 HRO, 6M50/25.
120 Ibid., 81M79M/E/1; 10M57 SP560; 21M65/F7/223/1 and 2.

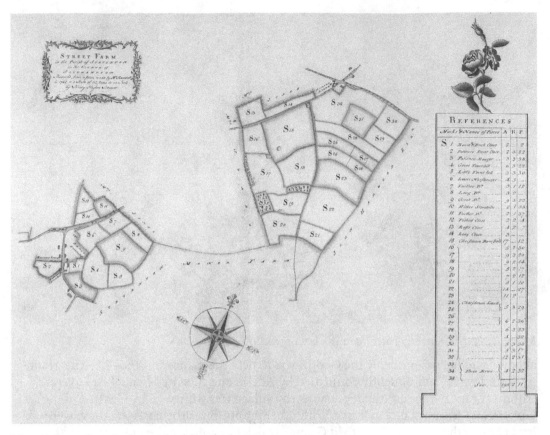

Map 10 *Street farm in the north of the parish, 1741.*

Queen's College Estate

In 1190, Michael de Luverez granted one yardland of land in Steventon to Monk
Sherborne prior, or to its mother house of St Vigor at Cerisy-la-Forêt (Dept. Manche,
Normandy) for the monks to pray for his soul and that of Margaret, his wife.[121] When the
priory was suppressed as an alien house in 1462, its lands were granted to the hospital
of God's House in Southampton, but because Edward III had given God's House to the
Queen's College, Oxford, they passed to the college.[122] The Revd William Knight gave 13s.
4d. a year to Queen's College as part of his Street farm leasehold from 1823 to 1860.[123]
This land was reserved from the sale to the duke of Wellington in 1855 and sold in 1860
to the Revd Gilbert Alder, who assumed responsibility for the 13s. 4d. payments.[124]

121 Bodleian Library, MS DD Queen's 241.
122 *VCH Hants.* II, 228.
123 HRO, 79M78/B213–4.
124 HRO, 39M89/E/B76; 68M72/DDZ14; 39M89/E/T26.

Lovers Alias Crooks Freehold

This freehold of 60 a. is an important minor estate which comprised land in the centre of the village and in the open fields. Its acquisition by the lord of the manor in 1736 was vital for his subsequent agricultural improvements. The origin of this freehold is unclear, but the de Luverez family were lords of the manor until the mid 13th century. It is probable that when the de Luverez quitclaimed Steventon to the des Roches,[125] they retained this small estate. In 1327 Andrew de Lovers paid 2s. and William Lovers paid 22d.[126] In 1512 a terrier recorded many pieces of land owned by William Lovers.[127] In 1525 two members of the family were assessed at £3 6s. 8d. and £2 respectively.[128] In 1586 William Lover paid 2s. 8d. subsidy on land valued at 40s.[129] The property passed to the Crook family in 1591 when William Lover bequeathed all his lands in Steventon and Ashe, to his daughter, Joan, the wife of John Crook, yeoman, of Steventon.[130] John Crook (d. 1616) provided that his son, Arthur, should be given sufficient timber to build himself a three-roomed house and barn on the copyhold, Uptons Hold.[131] He left all the rest of his estate, which included the Lovers alias Crookes two-yardland freehold (c.60 a.), to his wife, Joan, and his son, John. John owed money to a number of creditors,[132] and so sold his right in the two yardlands in Steventon and Ashe to his brother, Arthur. Arthur sold the land to Thomas Coteel who then sold it to his brother, Daniel, and Pierce Edgcumbe of Litchfield, Ashe, who sold it c.1637 to the Revd John Orpwood, rector of Steventon (1602–58).[133] Orpwood also purchased Pilgrims in Ashe.[134] After Orpwood's death, his widow, Joan, married the Revd John Harmar and they, supported by her daughter and son-in-law Elizabeth and Francis Powell, retained the freehold, claiming that Joan had rights for life in lieu of dower.[135] John Orpwood, born 1612, who followed his father as rector (1661–95) challenged this claim unsuccessfully, alleging that the Harmars had let the house fall into decay and chopped down the trees which surrounded and protected the dwelling house, barns and outhouses.[136] Joan and John Harmar died intestate in 1670 but Joan's daughter, Elizabeth Powell, who had moved into the freehold with her husband, Francis, before her mother's death, claimed a life interest and provoked another case brought by her brother, Revd John Orpwood, after which the property did eventually revert to the Orpwood male line.[137] Another John Orpwood, together with his widowed mother, Elizabeth Orpwood sold the property in 1712 to Sylvester Cuffley, yeoman of Overton, after whose death the land was sold to Edward Hooker and William

125 See p. 23.
126 *Hants. Tax List* 1327, 20.
127 TNA, E 368/438.
128 Ibid., E 179/173/183.
129 *Lay Subsidy*, 41.
130 HRO, 1591A/88. This was the same John Crook who supported Thomas Brocas in ejecting Sir Pexall Brocas from the Manor House.
131 HRO, 1616B/28.
132 Ibid., 18M61/box G/bundle 10.
133 Ibid., 18M61/box E/bundle 9; box G/bundle 10; 44M69/G4/1/39/14.
134 TNA, C 5/533/1.
135 Ibid., C 6/49/54.
136 Ibid., E 179/375/32; C 6/49/54.
137 Ibid., E 179/176/570; C 5/533/1.

Evelyn. Edward Hooker inherited the share of William Evelyn on Evelyn's death and sold all the property with land outside the parish for a total of £1,050 in 1728 to the Revd John Nicoll and Alice, his wife, who were living in Westminster in 1736, when they sold to Elizabeth Knight all their land in Steventon and Ashe for £1,300. The buildings and land in the parish of Steventon were valued at £700 and comprised a farmhouse (built about 25 years previously), two barns (one built ten years before) and a cart lodge which were all in pretty good repair. The land consisted of an orchard, 33 a. of inclosed land and 24 a. in the common fields with right of common for 40 sheep. In total the estate comprised 57 a. valued at £25 a year.[139] From the description recorded by Elizabeth Knight's surveyor, the freehold at the time of its purchase by the Knight family can be mapped (Map 8). The freehold from then was owned by the lords of the manor and merged with the main estate.

ECONOMIC HISTORY

IN 2015 STEVENTON WAS, as it always has been, a rural agricultural parish. Most of its land was owned by the lord of the manor until the late 20th century. In the Middle Ages, arable farming was mainly in open fields, but thereafter there was a process of piecemeal inclosure. Thus a survey of the lands of the church in 1512 shows the glebe lands scattered among the fields in long narrow strips, with each strip located with reference to tenants on either side. There were also some inclosed fields, although it is not clear whether these were old inclosures creating new fields out of common pasture or the product of inclosing pre-existing strips. Agriculture was mixed in character with sheep, pastured on the chalk downs in the south and west of the parish, being the main livestock. The open fields had been surrounded by large areas of open downland. The latter experienced encroachment in periods of population growth. In the 13th century this was seen in the development of Litchfield Grange and in the 16th in the expansionist policies of Pexall Brocas. Most of the pasture in the parish was in the southern half on the downs and used for grazing sheep. These poorer pastures would also have supported rabbits. The warren of Steventon was leased in 1636; no location was given but it was likely to be in the same area as Warren pond, recorded in 1758 and Warren Farm which included the pond and was leased from 1805 (Map 9).[1] Rabbit warrens and rough land amounting to 57 a. were sold with the manor in 1926.[2] Cattle were grazed on the lower, lusher pasture on clay soils in the north of the parish and their importance increased during the 20th century. There is no evidence of any communal meadow. There were 12 a. of meadow on Steventon Manor farm in 1757.[3] The new glebe created in 1824 out of Street farm included 3 a. of meadow in the centre of the parish.[4] In 1839 there were 74 a. of pasture and meadow; of this the 13 a. of pasture in the far north of the parish either side of the road to Deane was valued at 30s., double the value of the surrounding arable.[5] Cheesedown farm in the northern part of the parish, which was cut off in 1838 by the heavily embanked railway line, was sold separately by the second duke of Wellington, but the bulk of the estate remained intact until 1989 when it was divided and sold as freehold lots.[6]

Aside from agricultural changes, the 20th century saw the transformation of the village, as rural crafts disappeared, farms were enlarged and reduced in number and agricultural occupations ceased to dominate the village economy. In 2014 most of

1   HRO, 18M61/box E/bundle 9, tin box C, E. K. 2/box 2/bundle 20.
2   Ibid., 46M84/F86/3.
3   Ibid., 38M89/E/B561/4.
4   Ibid., 18M61/box 5/bundle 6. See p. 77.
5   Ibid., 18M61/box F/bundle 6.
6   See p. 49.

the villagers commuted to Basingstoke, Newbury or London or worked from home.[7] Commercial and light engineering businesses have developed to the east of the village since 1989.

Farming

Medieval Agriculture and Estate Management

The fragmentary evidence for medieval agriculture fits in with the general pattern of other villages in this area. In 1086 there was land for five ploughs with four plough teams, two held by the lord in demesne.[8] Then there were five villeins, three smallholders and the relatively large number of eight slaves, more than were needed to work the ploughs but they may have cared for sheep.[9] An Inquisition post mortem of 1277 showed the different elements of agriculture as reflected in the demesne lands of the lord. He possessed 360 a. of arable valued at 4d. an acre and downland pastures for 300 sheep, valued at 9s. a year. There was meadow land, and, as a later extent makes clear, some woodland.[10] No evidence survives of the cropping patterns but it was probably similar to the neighbouring manors of North Waltham or Herriard, with their large amounts of sown oats and a relatively small area of barley.[11] Agriculture was mainly carried out in open fields, which would have provided both arable and, when fallow, pasture land.

The lord, who held two carucates of land, probably leased out the demesne in the 12th century, and this was still the case in 1234, when Geoffrey des Roches was granted a licence to lease the demesnes.[12] He possessed a messuage (manor house) and garden, as well as his agricultural land and the lands of the village tenantry, both the free and the villein (bond) or customary tenants. In 1276 the free tenants generated rents of £5 2s. 2d. and, being over a quarter of the value of the manor; this constituted a particularly high figure in this area. The lord would have used hired labour as well as that of his tenants. The ten villeins then paid £3 12s. 4d. and they rendered work rents valued at £2 16s. 7d.[13] A later extent in 1361 shows similar elements, still with the chief messuage and various buildings, with a reduced arable acreage of 120 a., with pasture for 6 horses, 12 oxen and 300 sheep, 60 a. of woodland whose underwood was rented out, and the assized rents of free and bond tenants, now worth the reduced figure of £6 0s. 2d.[14] The importance of sheep to the medieval agricultural economy is demonstrated when John Champfor, a

7   Census, 2001: Steventon parish, distance travelled to work – Workplace Population, 2001 (UV80), http://www.neighbourhood.statistics.gov.uk (accessed 10 June 2015).
8   *Domesday*, 124.
9   Ibid., 124.
10   TNA, C 133/17/8; C 143/338/12.
11   J. Hare, 'The bishop and the prior: demesne agriculture in Medieval Hampshire', *Agricultural History Review*, 54 (2006), 196; idem, 'The nuns of Wintney Priory and their manor of Herriard: medieval agriculture and settlement in the chalklands of north-east Hampshire', *Proc. Hants. F.C.*, 70 (2015), 195–6.
12   *Cal. Pat. Henry III 1232–47*, 38.
13   TNA, C 133/17/8.
14   Ibid., C 143/338/12; *Cal. Inq. p.m*, XI, p. 166.

member of the local gentry died in 1409, leaving 417 sheep (237 wethers and 180 ewes) in Steventon out of a total of 3,354 sheep in six different places.[15]

Farming and Estate Management 1500–1700

From the early 16th century until 1633 lords of the manor resided in Steventon. Sir Richard Pexall in c.1538 and Sir Pexall Brocas from 1584 to 1611 tried to increase the value of their estate at the expense of the rights of their rectors and tenants. Land in the parish in the 16th century was divided into seven copyholds; a major freehold, known as Lovers alias Crookes with more than 60 a.; over 100 a. of freehold land belonging to Litchfield Grange, Ashe; a few small freehold and leasehold properties and the demesne farm, which was usually tenanted.[16] Copyholds were described in numbers of yardlands of 30 a.[17] A few tenants accumulated several holdings: in 1653 the main copyholder held three yardlands, made up of Hapsmales and Sonhangis and two half yardlands, Haywards and Spoores. He also held one pasture in Cheesedown, one toft called Spatenden and one croft called Isonhangers.[18] Another copyholder held two yardlands and the rest one each.[19] Some of Steventon was already inclosed in 1512 when six yardlands (measuring in this case, about 137½ a. in total) of glebeland were described as being in common fields and closes. Another c.40 a. of glebeland were mixed with the tenants' lands presumably in the common fields.[20] The 1512 survey also named some of the nine surviving open fields including Cockley Land, Westfield, Northfield, East Field, Whiteland, Hale Field and Twenton Field. These fields surrounded the main village settlement. The sheepdown also survived.

In c.1538 Sir Richard Pexall inclosed downland, on which his rector and tenants had common rights, to cultivate it himself. He deprived his rector of tithes and glebe, and his tenants of pasture, when he inclosed 300 a. of the Southdown but Sir Richard was ordered to restore the down to his rector and tenants.[21] The 14 surviving wills and seven inventories from the 16th century reveal mixed farming, with sheep being the main livestock.[22] In total the seven inventories (1559–94) valued sheep at £41, cattle at £27 and crops at £63. The average value of the inventories was £29, with a range from £9 to £40.[23] The will of Christopher Denby in 1528 left the largest flocks, bequeathing 204 sheep and 13 bullocks, more than were listed in any of the surviving inventories; and his family was already the most highly assessed in 1524–5.[24] There is no evidence to indicate whether Denby was a copyholder or the tenant of the Manor Farm. Daughters' dowries were provided in sheep; for example William Morall in 1546 left each of his daughters

15   BL Add. Ch. 26869.
16   HRO, 18M61/box E/bundle 9, box G/bundle 10.
17   Ibid., 18M61/box G/bundle 10, specifies that a yardland was 30 a.
18   Ibid., 18M61/box C/bundle 4.
19   Ibid.
20   TNA, E 368/438.
21   Ibid., C 78/3/98.
22   Steventon wills and inventories were read and transcribed by the VCH Hampshire wills group.
23   HRO, Steventon probate records.
24   HRO, 1528B/14; TNA, E 179/173/183. He also made by far the highest rent payment in the rental of the Pexall manor in 1549 (BL Add. Ch. 26560).

20 sheep.[25] The largest flock of sheep listed in an inventory was 101.[26] There was some indication of different types of flocks, as freeholder William Lover (d. 1591), possessed wethers, ewes and lambs valued at £4.[27] Some farmers used horses for ploughing with four inventories recording horses with harness and plough gear.[28] Others may still have used oxen. Christopher Denby (d. 1528) had 13 bullocks, including two ox-bullocks and one cow in 1528 and Richard Ayliffe (d. 1572), whose family were second most highly assessed in 1524–5, possessed six cows and three bullocks.[29] Most others had one cow for domestic use. Most inventories included pigs, hens, cocks, geese and ducks. The main crops of wheat and barley were equally divided in value, with some oats and fodder crops of peas and vetches also cultivated.

Estate management, after the death of Sir Richard Pexall in 1571, caused considerable conflict in the parish. The right of Sir Pexall Brocas to possess Beaurepaire and Steventon was contested by his grandfather's second wife, Lady Elinor,[30] leaving Sir Pexall to live mainly at Steventon for 28 years from 1583 to 1611. In the 1590s and the first decade of the 17th century Sir Pexall farmed his demesne directly, but he was accused of stealing land, crops, cattle and sheep from his tenants; three horses from the marquis of Winchester; profits from Thomas Beale of Ashe and 100 sheep and two rams from John Beale.[31] In 1613 a list of Sir Pexall's possessions was published after his son, Thomas, supported by local tenants, had forcibly removed his father from Steventon. This list, made in 1612, recorded 50 ewes great with lambs, 42 swine in the yard, and 40 wether sheep, 8 horses, 80 flitches of bacon, together with 50 a. of new sown wheat, to the value of £240 and £60 of provisions for his servants. He also had £500 worth of wheat, barley and other grain in the barn, but how much of it legitimately belonged to Sir Pexall is unknown.[32] One copyholder, Nicholas Ayliffe,[33] had complained in chancery in 1595 that Sir Pexall had caused Richard West and William Allen to disturb his possession of his tenement in Steventon and to impound his cattle.[34] Sir Pexall also caused his servants to steal corn from the barn of John Crook, a yeoman, who owned the Lovers alias Crookes 60 a. freehold and also held 60 a. of copyhold land.[35] The servants also stole barley which Crook had planted in his fields in c.1600. In alienating Ayliffe and Crook, he lost the support of two of the major families in the village. Pexall also impounded his neighbours' cattle, sheep and pigs after encouraging them to stray on to his land by removing fences.[36] In 1610 Lady Elinor and her third husband, Sir Robert Remington, were also accused by John Crook of taking away the messuage and 60 a., called Uptons Hold, which they had granted him c.1604 and for which he had paid £8 a year rent. Crook stated that they

25   HRO, 1546B/125.
26   Ibid., 1572B/005.
27   Ibid., 1591A/88.
28   Ibid., 1559A/056, 1568B/043, 1591A/061, 1591A/88.
29   Ibid., 1528B/14, 1572B/005. Denby also paid the highest customary rent payment in 1549 (BL, Add Ch. 26560).
30   See p. 25.
31   TNA, STAC 8/8/11.
32   Ibid., STAC 8/82/3.
33   Variants of this name were Aylif, Ayliff, Ayluf and Ailiffe.
34   TNA, C 2/Eliz/A5/47.
35   HRO, 1616B/028.
36   TNA, STAC 8/18/11.

falsely claimed that he was in arrears and granted the tenement and arrears to Richard Tompson.[37] Crook regained the land as copyhold from Sir Pexall's son, Sir Thomas.[38] The picture of Sir Pexall's activity accords with the evidence of four wills and nine inventories surviving from the first half of the 17th century. Altogether these have a total value of £564 and a range from £30 to £192.[39] The most valuable (£192) was that of John Crook (d. 1616). Sheep still dominated livestock and were valued at a total of £86 in the inventories. Cattle were valued at a total of £54 divided between five inventories. John Crook had the largest number possessing 10 cows and 7 bullocks valued at £30. Crook also produced butter and cheese.[40] He had six horses worth £30. Very few other inventories recorded horses. Wheat and barley continued to be important crops valued at a total of £112. Four of the inventories listed wool and four listed spinning wheels. Fodder crops of vetches, peas, oats, together with hay and straw were produced, valued in one inventory at £4 but usually at no more than £1. Six inventories listed butter, cheese and bacon.[41] Dung pots for manuring the fields also appeared in a third of the inventories.

From the mid 17th century the lords were increasingly absentee. The Manor farm was leased, together with copyhold rents, fines, heriots and wood profits. In 1658 total rents amounted to £371, including rent of £350 for the Manor farm, paid by John Brothers. The copyhold court in 1656 for example, yielded £66; woods brought in c.£20 a year.[42] After 1660 six inventories survive which again reveal a mixed farming economy with sheep, comprising ewes, lambs, wethers and tegs, continuing to be the main livestock. Charles Covey in 1661 left 49 sheep, fleece wool, lambs' wool and locks' wool together with scaffold, lugs and hurdles.[43] Fewer cattle were owned but all inventories contained wheat, barley and fodder crops. These inventories ranged in value from £53 to £1,099 for the inventory of Thomas Small, yeoman, in 1687.[44] However, £1,000 of Small's £1,099 related not to Steventon but to the valuation of land he held by lease for £48 a year in Basingstoke.[45] Wood, timber and faggots increasingly appeared in inventories. Open fields were mentioned in the glebe terrier of 1697 which listed, in addition to a close of glebe adjoining the parsonage house, a parcel of glebe lying in the Middle Common field by estimation ½ a.[46]

37   TNA, C 2/JasI/C28/66.
38   HRO, 1616B/028.
39   Ibid., 1608AD/26, 1613AD/002, 1616B/028, 1617A/74, 1625AD/3, 1626A/94, 1620AD/53, 1640A/196, 1614A/130, 1648AD/09.
40   Ibid.
41   Ibid.
42   Ibid., 18M61/box E/bundle 9.
43   Ibid., 1661B/19.
44   Ibid., 1670AD/122, 1676A/76, 1681B/57, 1689B/31. TNA, PROB 4/25564.
45   HRO, 1687AD/77.
46   Ibid., 21M65/E15/112.

Farming and Estate Management 1707–*c*.1855

Improving Landlords

At the beginning of the 18th century Steventon manor became part of the large Knight estate, managed from Godmersham in Kent, with property in London, Kent, Surrey and Chawton in Hampshire.[47] Initially in 1707, when William Knight inherited Steventon manor, little change was made in agricultural practice. The land he inherited was mainly inclosed but 236 a. was farmed in three open fields (Map 11) immediately north-west of the village. In 1736 the three fields were known as the Millway, Middle and Yonder fields[48] but they were also known as White Bread Field (77 a.), Brown Bread Field (58 a.) and Breadless Field (101 a.).[49] This residue of the common fields disappeared in 1741 when the lord of the manor used a private inclosure to convert the common fields into part of a new leasehold farm (Map 11).

The demesne or Manor farm (1,354 a.), occupying the centre and south of the parish, was leased to William Parker from 1731 for 11 years for £280 a year. A further farm, Street farm (195 a.), was divided into two parts, one (50 a.) of which lay in the centre of the village immediately north of the street containing the rectory (Maps 10 and 12); and the second part, Cheesedown lands (142 a.), lying in the far north of the parish, was leased to John Lovell, gentleman, for £45 a year.[50]

From 1736 the Knight landlords, although absentee, became very business-oriented as they restructured agricultural practice in Steventon by purchase, inclosure, lease covenants and management of the woods. This began in 1736 when Elizabeth Knight, widow of William, purchased the 60 a. freehold estate, Lovers alias Crookes, in the centre of the parish, from Dr Nicoll.[51] For £700 she acquired within Steventon a farm house, built about 25 years previously, two barns, one ten years old, a cart lodge, an orchard, 33 a. of inclosed land and 24 a. in the common field with right of common for 40 sheep; in total valued at £25 a year.[52] Following this purchase only 152 a. of freehold land adjoining the extreme south-west boundary of the parish remained independent of the lord of the manor. In 1738 Thomas Knight, a cousin of Elizabeth, inherited the estate and further enhanced his control by the purchase of the interests of five old copyholding families (Taplin, Woodruff, Crook, Lovell and Wheatley) in the open fields and closes, amounting to 166 a., together with their common pasture rights. Copyholders, for example Lovell's daughter in 1742, continued to rent houses and gardens into the 19th century[53] but the old family names slowly disappeared from the parish records, mainly as the male line

47   See p. 27.
48   HRO, 35M48/16/374; 39M89/E/B559/8. Middle Field retained its name in the tithe apportionment of
      1840. HRO, 21M65/F7/223/1.
49   HRO, 39M89/E/B/384.
50   Ibid., 39M89/E/B384/16; 587/20; 639/1.
51   See pp. 35–6.
52   HRO, 39M89/E/B559/1; 18M61/box G/bundle 10. The total purchase price was £1,300 which included
      seven closes in the neighbouring parish of Ashe. The purchase was recorded in the Court of Common
      Pleas.
53   HRO, 18M61/tin box C.

Map 11 *New or Bassetts farm, 1741, formed of the old ancient fields and the freeholds purchased by Elizabeth and Thomas Knight, 1736–41.*

died out. The deaths of Taplin, Lovell and Crook were recorded.[54] After these acquisitions the Steventon estate was leased for £446 a year.[55]

Until 1740 the lord of the manor, the main freeholder and five copyholders were permitted stints on the common fields and commons for a total of 350 sheep, of which 40 sheep were attached to Lovers alias Crookes freehold. The other stints ranged from 5 to 100 sheep.[56] Pasture for cattle was in the north of the parish on the lower lying ground. There is no evidence of communal cattle pastures or of stints for cattle on the open fields. By 1740 only one common pasture, Hazeldown Common or Sheepdown, of 22 a. existed. This adjoined the surviving open fields to the west of the village street. In the far south-west of the parish there appeared to be some 77 a. of rough sheep pasture in 1741, which by 1840 had become mainly arable with 16 a. of woodland.[57] The Manor farm in 1741

54   HRO, 71M82/PR 1.
55   Ibid., 39M89/E/B/559/11.
56   Ibid., 18M61/tin box C.
57   Ibid., 39M89/E/B/384; 21M65/F7/223/1.

had 44 a. of cow pasture (III on Map 12) lying a short distance north-east of the lane from the old rectory to the church.[58]

As a result of the purchases of freehold and copyhold land from 1736 to 1741, Thomas Knight was able in 1741 both to inclose the remaining 236 a. of common fields and combine these with Hazeldown Common to create a new leasehold farm, named New or Bassetts, after the first tenant. Bassetts farm comprised 325 a. in the north-west of the parish. The shapes of the three large fields extending to the north-west boundary of the parish are visible on contemporary maps (Map 11).[59] The new farm with the old copyhold closes extended in a northerly direction from the Hatch crossroads and behind the village street to the parish boundary in the north and west and adjoining Street farm on the east (a further 80 a. were in Ashe parish, just over the western boundary of Steventon).

Knight employed his Godmersham steward, Edward Randall, to survey and map all his estates, including these Steventon farms.[60] Knight then adjusted the farm sizes, transferring six Manor farm fields: Lower Down, Upper Down, Bottom Field, East Field, Lowance Field and Chalk Field, amounting in total to 272 a., together with 14 a. of the 44 a. of Manor farm cow pasture to Street/Cheesedown farm which was leased to Lovell.[61] This meant Manor farm (1067 a.) was leased for the reduced rent of £260, Street/Cheesedown farm (392 a.) was leased for £100 and the new/Bassetts farm (495 a.) for £125. The inclosure and rearrangement of farms led to a modest increase in annual rental value from £446 to £485.[62]

Knight both distrusted Hampshire farmers, including his tenants, and wanted to improve farming yields so he followed the practice adopted by many landowners at this time and introduced strict covenants into his farming leases.[63] When the new farm was leased to John Bassett of Steventon in September 1741,[64] the lease specified that to improve fertility, Hazeldown Common was to be ploughed up and chalk spread on each acre. All hay, straw and fodder were to be used on the land. Compost soil and dung were to be used in good husbandry style with all dung left in the farmyard in the last year of the lease. The first evidence of new fodder crops in Steventon was in these leases. At the end of his term Bassett had to leave 20 a. sown with sainfoin in good husbandlike manner not above four years growth, 40 a. sown with grass seeds not less than two, nor more than three years laid, and fitting for a wheat season in the new lease.[65] The lease recorded the recent changes in tenure resulting from the copyhold purchases when letting seven closes near the said house, described as 'five of which were late the estate of

58 HRO, 18M61/tin box C; shown as no. III and unnamed on HRO, 39M89/E/B384.
59 Ibid., 18M61/MP22; 39M89/E/B/384.
60 Ibid., 39M89/E/B/384.
61 Ibid., 18M61/tin box C compared with HRO, 39M89/E/B384/16-17.
62 Ibid., 39M89/B559/11. These valuations both included the seven fields in Ashe attached to the new farm which were not valued separately.
63 HRO, 39M89/E/B/561/4. See for example, R.A.C. Parker, *Coke of Norfolk: a Financial and Agricultural Study* (Oxford, 1975) and J.R. Wordie, *Estate Management in the Eighteenth Century: the Building of the Leveson Gower Fortune* (1982).
64 HRO, 18M61/E. K. 2/box 2/bundle 20.
65 Ibid.

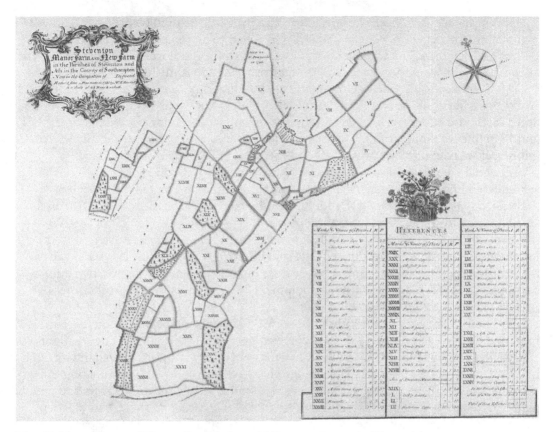

Map 12 *Manor farm and New or Bassetts farm, 1741, occupying most of the parish.*

Clemence Taplin, widow, and two of Henry Woodruff'.[66] Timber, together with the rights
to hunt and shoot, was reserved to the use of the landlord.

In reality some of Knight's tenants faced financial problems in the mid 18th century.
In 1743 tenants were reported to have lost money for the preceding three years[67] and
the tenant of Manor farm, Hellier, was bankrupt by 1758. Knight accused Hellier,
together with other Hampshire farmers, of robbing the farm of all he could and leaving
the landlord to repair the damage. In particular Knight had given Hellier permission
to grub up and plough the wood but Hellier had only sold the timber. Also Hellier
had failed to fold adequate sheep on the farm in the last year of his tenancy.[68] Knight
subsequently leased Manor and Bassetts farms to Richard Digweed, after John Bassett
had died childless in 1758 and his farm, now described as Little Farm, was combined
with Manor Farm (now referred to as Great Farm) in a lease to Richard Digweed, the
elder and Richard Digweed the younger of Sydmonton (Hants.) for £308 a year. Knight
had reservations about letting Bassetts with the Great or Manor farm, as the horse
teams would be kept at the manor, so the land of Bassetts might not be well manured.

66   HRO, 18M61/E. K. 2/box 2/bundle 20.
67   Ibid., 18M61/box C.
68   Ibid., 21M65/C9/414; in 1750 Hellier was involved in a tithe dispute in Kingsclere where he failed to pay
     the tithes on 305 a. he farmed.

The lease thus required both the Great farm and the Little farm to be properly fallowed and manured by a summer sheep fold. The crops had to be rotated and were to include fallows and sainfoin. The woodlands were reserved to the landlord.[69] The Digweeds were effective tenants who dominated the economy of Steventon until 1877.[70]

The Knights also invested in improving the buildings and services of their tenancies. In 1741 two barns in the southern part of Manor farm, known as Warren, were rebuilt and a carthouse added.[71] The field pattern of Warren farm was transformed between 1741 and 1840 into rectangular fields which had the appearance of parliamentary inclosure but in fact was the result of private improvement, on either side of a new road.[72]

The Revd George Austen was a tenant of the Knights. William Hellier had surrendered his tenement and close of 4 a. so that it could be granted to Revd George Austen (Map 6, field number 47), soon to become father of Jane Austen (b. 1775), as a small holding to supplement his clerical income.[73] Austen was also tenant of the 200 a. of Cheesedown farm where he reared pigs and sheep.[74] When George Austen moved his family from Steventon to Bath in 1801, he sold his farm stock of three cows and calves, five cart-horses, three sows, 22 pigs, seven store pigs, three market wagons, two dung carts, four ploughs and other farming equipment.[75] Unlike most of the local farmers, Austen did not possess sheep.

On Thomas Knight's death without issue in 1794, Edward Austen, brother of Jane, inherited the Knight estate and in 1812 changed his name to Knight.[76] Austen/Knight was an absentee (living at Godmersham or Chawton) but active landlord, managing through his estate stewards. In 1798 mixed farming continued with sheep still dominating the pastoral side. In 1798 1,100 sheep were recorded in the parish but only 5 cows and 64 pigs. There were 34 draught horses, 12 waggons and five carts and there were stores of 380 qr of wheat, 250 qr of barley, 220 loads of hay and 50 qr of vetches. The parish had 20 ovens in which 60 bushels of wheat could be made into bread each week.[77] By 1800 the Knights had constructed wheat, barley and oat barns, as well as granary, carthouse and stables at Manor and Bassetts Farms.[78] A new pond was constructed for Bassetts Farm at a cost of £39 at the request of the tenant as his sheep lacked water. This was built on part of the one-time copyhold mead purchased by Knight from Woodruff. Into the 19th century, leases stated that the landlord would provide building materials and pay half the costs of craftsmen to keep all property repaired.[79] This was done with payments to tradesmen including carpenters, masons and bricklayers.[80] In 1801, 267 a. of wheat, 250

69   HRO, 39M89/E/B/622; 18M61/E. K. 2/box 2/bundle 20.
70   Ibid., 1739B/32; 18M61/E. K. 2/box 2/bundle 20.
71   Ibid., 18M61/tin box C/bundle 7.
72   See Map 4, p. 9.
73   HRO, 18M61/E. K. 2/box 2/bundle 20.
74   Ibid.; Austen *Letters*, 24, 38.
75   *Reading Mercury,* notices of auctions, 4 May 1801, 14 Sept. 1801.
76   *VCH Hants.* IV, 172.
77   HRO, Q22/1/2/5/10.
78   Ibid., 18M61/E. K. 2/box 2/bundle 20.
79   For example, HRO, 18M61/E. K. 2/box 2/bundle 20. Lease of Warren farm, 21 March 1806.
80   HRO, 79M78/B211–3.

a. of barley, 250 a. of oats, 60 a. of turnips or rape, 28 a. of rye, 12 a. of peas and 1½ a. of potatoes were grown.[81]

The main revenue of the estate came from the rents of the tenanted farms. In 1805 Warren farm (345 a.) was divided from Manor farm and let with Cheesedown farm (141 a.) to Thomas Waldron of Deane for £234 a year and the total income from rents of these farms amounted to £439 in 1809.[82] Warren farm was leased separately from Cheesedown farm in 1812 to Robert Hall for £165 a year. Robert Hall went bankrupt in 1816, after which the landlord had to spend £135 on ploughing and seed corn before leasing it to Richard Twitchen for 1s. rent for the first year, rising to £100 and finally £150 a year, from the second year of the lease.[83] The continuing importance of sheep farming and folding was illustrated by the hurdles and sheep cages owned by the tenant of Warren farm in 1816. Warren farm was chalked and wheat, grass and turnips were cultivated. Cheesedown farm grew wheat, barley, turnips, sainfoin and grass, providing both cash and fodder crops.[84] The Digweeds invested in technology c.1800, building a threshing mill powered by four horses.[85] From 1831 Aaron Gale, tenant of Warren farm, was required to pen and fold 150 ewes on the land each year or 200 dry sheep and lambs. He also had to plant 30 a. with turnips, which should similarly be penned and folded with sheep.[86]

The agricultural estate was further rearranged in 1824 to provide an additional 50 a. of glebe land for William Knight, son of Edward, who became rector in 1823.[87] This comprised the land adjoining the village street from the crossroads to North Waltham where the old rectory and adjoining cottages had stood (Map 13) and nearly 30 a. taken out of Manor farm, together with 20 a. from Street farm. The glebe land thus lay either side of the old village street. The rest of Street farm (40 a.), including the farmhouse, was leased to the Revd William Knight.[88] This arrangement lasted until 1931 when the rectory was sold.[89]

However, despite the work of landlords and tenants, productivity was low in the parish in 1839, with poor husbandry, the tilth full of weeds and switch grass 'as though it was the intention of the farmer to obtain a crop of weed rather than of corn'.[90] The crops were wheat, turnips and oats and two leys which were poorish in quality and moderate in quantity'. The land was reported to be 'susceptible of vast improvement'.[91] Cheesedown Farm was temporarily in hand in 1839, possibly because the railway embankment had cut it off from the rest of the parish and Edward Knight suggested a reduction in rent to attract a tenant.[92] The farm comprised 121 a. of arable valued at 15s. an acre, 13 a. of pasture valued at 30s. per acre, together with 16 a. of hedgerows valued at 10s. an acre.

81   Le Faye, *Steventon*, 42–3; TNA, HO 67/24.
82   HRO, 18M61/E. K. 2/box 2/bundle 20; 79M78/B211.
83   HRO, 79M78/B211; E. K. 2/box 2/bundle 20.
84   HRO, 39M89/E/B238/7.
85   Le Faye, *Steventon*, 11–12.
86   HRO, 18M61/E. K. 2/box 2/bundle 20.
87   See pp. 77–8.
88   HRO, 21M65/F7/223/1; 79M78/B212.
89   *The Times*, 14 Aug. 1931.
90   TNA, IR 18/9144.
91   Ibid.
92   HRO, 18M61/E. K. 2/box 2/bundle 20; 21M65/F7/223/1.

To this Knight added the 46 a. of East Field, valued at 13s. an acre which was cut off from Manor farm and lay between Cheesedown lands and the railway embankment.[93] The whole was valued at £148 a year but Knight leased it for £140, firstly to the Rector, William Knight, and then to Abraham Davis, then in 1852 to Dennis Taylor.[94]

Agriculture c.1855–2016

In 1855 Edward Knight (born 1798) who had inherited his father Edward's estate in 1852 sold it to Arthur Richard Wellesley, second duke of Wellington, who owned it until 1877. Land ownership by Wellington had very little impact on Steventon. In 1855 Manor farm was leased to Mr William Francis Digweed for £625 a year, Warren farm to the Revd John Digweed for £50, Street farm to Revd William Knight for £26 (he also paid £49 for cottages).[95] The Digweeds continued as tenants of the Manor farm with the terms of their lease unchanged when it was renewed in 1863 for 14 years at £900 a year. Shooting rights were reserved to the landlord. Repairs to tenants' property continued to be part-funded by the landlord and the woods were managed[96] but his steward could not even produce copies of the Digweed lease when Wellington wanted to sell the estate in 1877.[97]

In 1851 William Francis Digweed, tenant of Manor farm, farmed 1,004 a. and employed 18 workers, including a bailiff, a shepherd and five carters. Within the parish there was one other shepherd, two gamekeepers and 30 agricultural labourers and carters. By 1859 Digweed's nephew, Revd John James Digweed, farmed 380 a. of Warren farm where he employed seven workers, including a bailiff and three boys, while he lived at Manor Farm. Dennis Taylor farmed Cheesedown farm. By 1875 he was also bailiff for Revd John Digweed at Warren Farm.[98] Taylor was succeeded by H. J. Hughes at Cheesedown Farm.[99] In 1861 William F. Digweed employed 22 labourers and 9 boys. Cheesedown farm comprised 198 a., where five labourers and two boys were employed. In 1861 there were 22 carters in the parish, a considerable increase.[100] In 1871 John Digweed, nephew of William (d. 1863) and tenant of Manor farm, completely dominated the economy of the village. He farmed 1,380 a. and employed 38 (29 men and nine boys). In total there were 51 farm workers in the parish, made up of 42 agricultural labourers and carters, six shepherds and two bailiffs.[101] In the same year, out of the 2,155 a. in the parish 1,648 a. were arable, 130 a. were pasture and 252 a. were woods.[102] Sheep remained important throughout the late 19th century, although the number of shepherds dropped to five in 1881 and four in 1891.[103] In 1901 there were 14 agricultural labourers, nine carters and four cattlemen, four shepherds, one bailiff, one farm foreman

93 HRO, box F/bundle 6. The valuation for pasture sounds very high in comparison with the arable but the reason for this is not stated.
94 HRO, 79M78/B213.
95 HRO, 79M78/B213.
96 MERL, Wellington/273/1-17.
97 Ibid., Wellington/1621, 1622.
98 Census 1851; *White's Dir. Hants. & IOW* (1859), 514; *Kelly's Post Office Dir.* (1867), 672; (1875), 224.
99 *White's Dir. Hants.* (1878), 582.
100 Census 1861.
101 Census 1871; HRO, 5M62/6, page 474 (microfilm M249).
102 OS area book, 1872.
103 Census 1881, 1891.

and three gamekeepers who reflected the increased importance of shooting rights. The woods continued to be important with three woodmen employed.[104] In 1901 sheep still dominated with 1,400 but numbers of cattle (125) were increasing. There were also 155 pigs.[105]

Henry Harris who had purchased Steventon in 1877 became the first resident landowner for 240 years. He modernised the estate, aided by his bailiff, William Mattick, and built a new manor house and houses for estate workers. Bassetts farm was provided with a new large farmhouse and brick barns replaced the dilapidated buildings in the manor grounds and at Bassetts.[106] Cheesedown farm had been sold separately by Wellington to Mr Beach in 1877[107] and by 1895 was owned by John and Henry Fooks.[108] The son of Henry Harris, also Henry, inherited the main estate of 1,632 a. on his father's death in 1898. Harris sold the manor, including Bassetts farm (882 a.) leased for £600 a year and Warren farm (369 a.) leased for £200 a year, to Robert Mills in 1910.[109] Mills also acquired Litchfield Stud Farm, mainly in Ashe but including 64 a. in Steventon, which was leased to a member of the British Bloodstock Agency.[110] In 1912 the estate also leased 5 a. of allotment gardens (Map 7) immediately north-west of the houses on the Triangle extending to the railway line in the area where the last surviving open fields had been situated.[111] In the first half of the 20th century, the economy of the parish was still agricultural. The two main farms, Bassetts (882 a.), tenanted by Walter Cann for £600 a year, and Warren (369 a.), tenanted by F. and C. Shirvell for £200 a year, were mostly arable with dairy cows, piggeries and cart-horse stabling at Bassetts.[112] In 1911 25 out of 57 heads of household were involved in farming. The increased importance of cattle was illustrated with equal numbers of cowmen (4) as shepherds (4).[113]

By 1923 the manor house was unoccupied and the glebe had become a farm occupied by Mrs George Stone.[114] Jack Onslow Fane purchased the estate in 1926 and inhabited the manor house. At this time the agricultural estate was let as two farms: Bassetts and Warren, which comprised 1,400 a. in Steventon and 40 a. in Ashe. Both farms were let to F. Bloomfield for £800 a year.[115] The estate agent lived in Steventon Firs bungalow. In addition the estate leased one cottage and one bungalow for £7 and £40 a year respectively. Eleven acres of pasture inclosures were let for £9 a year and the allotment gardens were let to ten holders for £2 7s. 6d. a year.[116] Jack Onslow Fane introduced pedigree animals: Shorthorn cows, Hampshire Down sheep and Large White pigs, which he auctioned in 1936 when he sold the manor to the Hutton Crofts.[117]

104 Census 1901.
105 TNA, MAF 68/1325.
106 *Kelly's Dir. Hants.* (1889), 445.
107 MERL, Wellington/1622-4.
108 *Kelly's Dir. Hants.* (1895), 520.
109 HRO, 62A00/1.
110 Ibid., 46M84/F86/3.
111 OS Map 1:2500, Hants. XXV. 4 (1912 edn).
112 HRO, 62A00/1.
113 Census 1911.
114 *Kelly's Dir. Hants.* (1923), 638.
115 HRO, 46M84/F86/3.
116 Ibid.
117 G. Goddard, *Steventon in the 1930s* (1995), 21–2; Le Faye, *Steventon*, 14.

Figure 17 *Pasture on the slopes below the church in 2014.*

In 1941 the main farming units were Steventon or Bassetts farm (1,100 a.), tenanted by Captain Shirra Gibb and Home farm and Warren farm (483 a.), based at Warren farm, owned by Captain B. Hutton Croft of the Old Rectory who was described as a stock and grass farmer. Cheesedown farm comprised 259 a., where the agent was described as lacking in experience of arable farming. The main crops were oats (350 a.), followed by wheat (169 a.) and barley (131 a.). A few acres were also sown with potatoes, turnips, mangolds and kale. The main land use was increasingly grazing and fodder crops (919 a.) for the developing cattle industry. Livestock consisted of 238 cows, one bull and 1,217 sheep. Hutton Croft also owned Steventon Piggeries which possessed 351 pigs. Peak Hill House (0.25 a.), immediately north of the railway line and west of Steventon Arch, had 1,200 poultry. There were six tractors, four of them on Home and Warren farms.[118]

Dairy farming increased steadily from 1866 when there were 40 cattle and in 1872 when there were 103 a. of pasture.[119] Most of this land was concentrated on the slopes east of the village street extending uphill to the church, some distance south of the pasture grazed in 1741.[120] By 1840 the main pasture (38 a.) was on the slopes (Fig. 17) down from the church to the village street and in the far north of the parish surrounding Cheesedown Farm (15 a.).[121] During the 20th century, cattle replaced sheep as the main livestock. In 1926 Bassetts farm had accommodation for 70 cows[122] and from 1939

118   TNA, MAF 32/990/76.
119   Ibid., MAF 68/28.
120   OS Area book 1872.
121   HRO, 21M65/F7/223/1 and 2.
122   Ibid., 159M88/1590.

this farm specialized in Friesian cattle.[123] Numbers of cattle, especially for milk, in the parish increased steadily with 244 in 1941, grazing 306 a. of permanent pasture.[124] There were 380 cattle in 1961, 511 (of which 339 were milk cows grazing 700 a. of permanent pasture) in 1971, and 413 in 1981.[125] Bassetts farm's Friesians were crossed with Holsteins from 1970 to produce more milk for the Milk Marketing Board. In 2013 milk was purchased by Dairy Crest to supply Marks and Spencer. Sheep numbers in the parish, by contrast, fell from a peak of about 1,500 in the late 19th century to 300 in 1981.[126] When the estate was broken up from 1987 to 1989, the tenants bought Warren and Bassetts Farms. Nurshanger and Stoken Farms developed on Frog Lane with mixed farming but also a commercial/light industrial development.[127] In 2014 agriculture was mainly arable and dairy farming with woodland used for shooting and coppicing.

Woodland

Woodland throughout the parish was the property of the lord of the manor and was managed by his estate. During the Middle Ages, woods were apparently fairly extensive. In 1260, Geoffrey des Roches purchased half of Steventon but promised the vendors, Geoffrey and Egelina, 12 cartloads of wood annually from his Steventon woods for life.[128] This woodland was not recorded in 1277 but woods extended to 60 a. in 1361 when the underwood was worth 4s. a year.[129] By the 17th century the landlord leased out the woodland with the Manor farm. In c.1648 the tenant enjoyed rights of pasture and feeding in the woods on his leasehold land. In 1741 the rights were reclaimed from the tenants and the woodland was managed in hand by the new landlords as part of their transformation of estate management. [130] New leases excluded woods and underwoods, reserving them to the private use of the lord of the manor for timber, bark and faggot sales and, increasingly, for shooting and hunting.[131] In 1838, out of 179 a. of woodland, 163 a. were managed in hand by the estate, mainly in five coppices (128 a.) dispersed to the south of the village. These were Hazeldown, Crawley, Cowage, Ashen Grove and Misholt. Knight sold timber in Steventon worth £550 17s. 4d. (1854) and £502 10s. 9d., just before he sold the estate to the second duke of Wellington.[132] In 1855 the woods preserved partridges, hares and pheasants for 'gentleman fond of sporting'.[133]

The estate profited from wood sales throughout the 19th century and the value of woodland caused the acreage of managed woodland to expand into the 20th century. Sales of oak and ash trees, bark and faggots yielded on average £146 a year from 1808 to 1819.[134] In 1831, 22 a. were excluded from the new lease of Warren farm to extend the

123 TNA, MAF 68/28.
124 Ibid., MAF 32/990/76.
125 Ibid., MAF 68/3979, 4724, 5224, 5750.
126 Ibid., MAF 68/28, 755, 1325, 1895, 2465, 3026, 3566, 3979, 4349, 4724, 5224, 5750.
127 Le Faye, *Steventon,* 19.
128 TNA, CP 25 204/10/31.
129 Ibid., C 143/338/12; C 133/17/8.
130 HRO, 18M61/box E/bundle 9; 39M89/E/B/384.
131 Ibid., 18M61/E. K. 2/box 2/bundle 20.
132 Ibid., 79M78/B213.
133 Ibid., 10M57/SP639. See p. 64.
134 HRO, 79M78/B211; 10M57/SP645.

woodland west from Misholt Coppice to create Cocksford Plantation along the southern boundary of the parish.[135] Woodland covered 179 a. in 1838, 252 a. in 1872, 227 a. in 1908 and 297 a. in 1926.[136] In 1891 three woodmen were employed in the parish, but by the 20th century the woodland was mainly used for shooting.[137] In 2011 most of the 250 a. of woodland was attached to Steventon Warren farm. It was managed by a gamekeeper and let for shooting in the season.[138]

Industry, Crafts, Commerce and Services

William Savage of Steventon was a rich merchant who, with two others, could lend £2,000 in the early 14th century.[139] The woollen cloth industry survived in Hampshire in the 16th and early 17th century but the surviving evidence of this from Steventon is very limited. In the late 20th century there was diversification into light industry and commerce in a small area of the parish. Traditional village crafts were also present.

Rural Crafts

In the 16th century sheep were the dominant livestock in the parish and Steventon would have been a wool-producing parish, but there is very little evidence of cloth production. Wool was recorded in one will and two inventories but none of the 16th-century inventories included spinning wheels.[140] There is a hint of trading in wool in the will of Edward Hellier (d. 1591), as Robert Bendall of Westbury (Wilts.) (an important cloth producing town), held 94 pounds of wool belonging to Hellier.[141] From the early 17th century more evidence survives of the processing of wool adding value to the raw material. Four of the inventories recorded spinning wheels and four possessed wool[142] but more significantly Richard Woodruff (d. 1641) left 10s. to 'the poorest sort of spinners which usually come to my house for spinning work'.[143] After 1660 no inventories included spinning wheels but three listed wool.[144] There was little evidence of other trades and crafts before the 18th century, apart from a carpenter (d. 1533), who bequeathed to his servant all the tools of his trade, including timber, axe and a lathe.[145] In the Middle Ages brewers were fined for breaking regulations controlling ale sales. There was usually only a single brewer but sometimes more than one.[146]

From the late 18th century until the 1930s the village had a blacksmith who often served for long periods of time: George Bone worked from 1859 to 1889 and John

---

135 HRO, 18M61/E. K. 2/box 2/bundle 20; OS Map 1:10560, sheet XXV (1872 edn).
136 HRO, 21M65/F7/223/1; OS area book 1872; HRO, 46M84/F86/3.
137 Census, 1891; HRO, 62A00/1.
138 The information about Warren farm was a personal communication from the owner, Peter Harrison, and Richard Tanner, 14 Nov. 2011.
139 TNA, C 241/119/175; C 241/118/20.
140 HRO, 1535B/34, 1559A/056/1, 1591A/061.
141 Ibid., 1591A/061.
142 Ibid., 1613AD/1617A/74, 1625/AD/33/1, 1620AD/53/1, 1640A/196/1, 1641A/130.
143 Ibid., 1641A/130.
144 Ibid., 1661B/19/2, 1670AD/122, 1676A76/2.
145 Ibid., 1533B/30.
146 Ibid., 148M71/2/1/34, 2/1/4; 2/1/34; 2/1/65, 2/7/1; 2/7/2; Baigent and Millard, *Basingstoke*, 395.

Gascoigne from 1911 to 1931.[147] The blacksmith was joined by a carpenter in 1851 and a carpenter-wheelwright by 1875.[148] Clothing trades were represented by a tailor and a plush weaver in 1792.[149] Management of the woods in hand provided employment for woodmen, sawyers and a bailiff during the late 18th and 19th centuries. Charles Littleworth was bailiff in 1835 and Charles Englefield was a sawyer.[150] A woodman was employed to manage the woods and coppices, responsible for hedgerows, felling trees, stripping bark and making faggots.[151] By 1920 there was also a wood dealer.[152]

In 1851 other trades included a brush manufacturer and a shoemaker, George Smith. By 1861 Smith's shoemaking business had expanded and he employed one man and two apprentices and was described as shoemaker, shopkeeper and postmaster.[153] In 1871 Smith lived at the post office and employed three men in his boot- and shoemaking business. By 1878 George Soper, who was listed as a journeyman shoemaker in 1881, was the bootmaker and postmaster while Smith remained a grocer. Mrs Elizabeth Bone was a dressmaker.[154] Construction of Henry Harris's new mansion house temporarily increased the village craftsmen in 1881: ten plasterers, seven carpenters, two joiners and one bricklayer were employed. There was also a machinist employing six men who may have been working on the mansion.[155] Herbert Ranger was established as a haulage contractor by 1939.[156]

Milling

There is no evidence of the medieval lords possessing a mill, and fines for milling are rare. Milling could have been done outside the village, by hand or by horse, but two millers were recorded in 1415 and one in 1422.[157] Much later in 1851, George Hutt was described as a miller but with no indication of any mill construction. By 1861 he had expanded his business and was described as a miller and grocer living at Mill Green shop at Deane Gate with his wife, Jane, also described as a miller, his five children and a servant or miller's man.[158] There is no further mention of a miller and by 1871 the Hutt family had moved to Eastrop mill, just east of Basingstoke.

Retail and Services

At the end of the 18th century, fabrics and drapery goods could be purchased from the Overton Scotchman, a local pedlar.[159] A few retail outlets developed in the 19th century.

---

147 HRO, 1779A/114, 1812AD/64; *White's Dir. Hants.*, 1859, 514; Census 1851.
148 *Post Office Dir. Hants.* (1875), 224.
149 HRO, 1792A/19.
150 Ibid., 1836B/17.
151 Ibid., 79M78/B211.
152 *Kelly's Dir. Hants.* (1920), 598.
153 *Kelly's Post Office Dir. Hants.* (1867), 672; Census 1871, 1881.
154 *White's Dir. Hants.* (1878), 582.
155 Census 1881.
156 *Kelly's Dir. Hants.* (1939), 540.
157 HRO, 148M71/2/1/15; 2/7/1.
158 Census 1851, 61.
159 Austen, *Letters*, 22.

In 1832 George Smallbone was a shopkeeper.[160] In 1848 James Hutt was a mealman.[161] His widow, Mary Hutt in 1849 was described as a shopkeeper.[162] In 1851 there were two grocers, one baker and a beerseller and the pub at Deane Gate. Esther Church was described as a beerhouse keeper in 1911.[163] In 1901 George Soper was still living in the post office but his wife was the postmistress.[164] In the 20th century the post office, at 1 Stonehills from 1926 (Map 7), was also a general store. From 1939 to 1945 the post office and shop was run from North Waltham by Victor Rosenthal. Miss Lytle then ran a post office and shop until 1977.[165] A fortnightly village shop ran in the village hall on alternate Saturdays from 1983 to 1998. In 2013 there was only a mobile shop.

Employment on the Railway

Within the parish there was a signal box and local men worked on the railway by 1851.[166] Two men were employed as railway labourers in 1871.[167] By 1881 four platelayers and two signalmen lived in Steventon, together with two engine drivers who lived near the railway. By 1891 ten railway workers lived in the parish: two signalmen, seven platelayers, all working for L&SWR, and a clerk. In 1901 and 1911 there were nine rail workers, mainly platelayers and signalmen.[168] The signal box itself was sited to the north of the line and resembled a platelayer's hut, consisting of a single storey wooden structure built on top of the embankment. It was closed and demolished in 1966 as part of the electrification and accompanying resignalling of the main line to Southampton and Bournemouth by British Rail.[169]

Light Industry and Commerce from the Late 1980s

After the break-up of the estate (1986–9) the economy diversified, with some commercial and light industrial development east of the village on Frog Lane at Stoken and Nurshanger Farms, including in 2014 workshops in which light aircraft were restored. These new businesses sold security equipment, exhibition services, broadband provision, catering equipment and leased heavy plant. Just north of Popham airfield was a commercial site with vehicle workshops.[170]

---

160 HRO, 1832AD/95.
161 Ibid., 1848A/55.
162 Ibid., 5M62/3/278.
163 OS Map 1:10560, Hants. XXV (1872 edn); Census 1851.
164 Census 1901.
165 Tanner, *Steventon*, 21.
166 Census 1851.
167 Census 1871.
168 Census 1881–1911.
169 E. Course, *The Railways of Southern England: the Main Lines* (1973), 255.
170 Personal observation, 2014.

The Village Community 1350–1550

THE RELATIVE SPREAD OF taxable wealth in the parish is apparent in the assessment for the subsidy of 1524–5.[1] The two wealthiest members of the village were Peter Denby assessed at £40, and Richard Ayliffe assessed at £30, with the next at £10. Below this there was an even spread down to the four taxpayers who were assessed at the minimum of £1, although some may have been too poor to be assessed at all. Both the Ayliffe and Denby families were substantial influences in the village. John Ayliffe was one of the assessors in 1512, Richard Ayliffe was the second most highly assessed taxpayer in 1524 and paid substantially the highest rent in 1549.[2] In addition to Peter Denby in 1524–5, a William Denby was assessed at 26s. 8d.[3] Christopher Denby (d. 1528) was a wealthy farmer with servants.[4] Both the Ayliffes and the Denbys were families who were also prominent elsewhere in the nearby parishes, such as Deane and Overton, whether as large-scale farmers or as cloth traders.[5] Half of the 16th century testators had servants.[6]

Social Structure 1550–c.1740

Sir Richard Pexall began the rebuilding of the manor house from c.1560 to 1571. Sir Pexall Brocas was resident from 1584 to 1611 but he alienated rather than led the local community.[7] A Star Chamber case in 1605 revealed many alleged crimes against his servants and tenants. Sir Pexall had many illegitimate children and kept not only his wife in the manor house but also 'lewd women', some of whom he compelled his servants to marry once he had made them pregnant. He had also impregnated many local women.[8] He was succeeded by his son, Sir Thomas Brocas, whose three children were born in the parish between 1615 and 1619.[9] However, in 1626, Sir Thomas Brocas regained his main family manor of Beaurepaire and left Steventon which he sold to Thomas Coteel,

1   TNA, E 179/173/183.
2   Ibid., E 368/438; E 179/173/183; BL Add. Ch. 26579, 26560.
3   TNA, E 179/173/183.
4   HRO, 1528B/14. For a fuller discussion of Denby see Economic History.
5   J. Thirsk, 'The farming regions of England', *Agrarian Hist. England* (4), 65; TNA, E 101/347/17; HRO, 1544U2/1, 1569P/06, 1543U/2, 1549B/04.
6   Ibid., Steventon probate 1528–99; http://www.victoriacountyhistory.ac.uk/explore/items/steventon-probate-material-1500-1700 (accessed 6 Nov. 2015).
7   See pp. 40, 84.
8   TNA, STAC 8/8/11.
9   HRO, 71M82/PR1. Elizabeth, daughter of Mr Thomas Brocas, was baptized 24 March 1615; Prudence, daughter, was baptized 14 Oct. 1617 and Thomas, son, was baptized 29 March 1619.

a wealthy London merchant, who resided in Steventon from 1626 to 1633. Coteel also purchased other properties in Hampshire, Lancashire, Essex and London. Coteel was MP for Camelford (Cornw.) from 1625; his brother-in-law, Piers Edgcumbe, being a substantial landowner in Cornwall.[10] Coteel loaned £20 to Charles I in 1626 as part of the forced loans of that year and was High Sheriff of Hampshire in 1630.[11] From 1633 Steventon once more ceased to be the main residence of its lords of the manor. Sir Thomas Brocas lived at Beaurepaire, the Mynnes and the Evelyns in Epsom and the Lewknors in West Sussex. The Lewknors kept Steventon Manor House as a secondary residence and, initially with the Evelyns, held courts there until 1700.[12] The Manor farm was leased to John Brothers by 1648 and perhaps before.[13]

The rector and the leading farmers were also active in local society. The rector from 1602 to 1658 was John Orpwood.[14] John Crook (d. 1616) was the main freeholder with 60 a. of freehold and *c*.60 a. of copyhold land. The overseers of Crook's will were the lord of the manor and the rector, reflecting Crook's own importance in the community. His inventory was valued at £193.[15] Richard Ayliffe, a leading copyholder, had an estate valued at £47 in 1572 but his family seems to have died out shortly after this.[16]

In 1665 13 households were taxed for a total of 42 hearths. Sir John Lewknor and his wife, Anne, held the manor house which had ten hearths. The rector, John Orpwood, had succeeded his father in 1661 after a short gap.[17] The Orpwoods, between 1624 and 1665, had purchased the main freehold, Lovers alias Crookes (60 a.) which included a nine-hearth farmhouse; in the 18th century this became part of Bassetts farm. In 1665 the Revd John Orpwood was living in the three-hearth rectory, while his widowed mother, Joanne, who had married the Revd John Harmar, as her second husband, inhabited the nine-hearth farmhouse.[18] John Harmar was a clergyman and Greek and Latin scholar who had been ordained in 1617. He served as Master of St Albans School and Under Master at Westminster School before becoming Regius Professor of Greek at Oxford in 1650. Harmar published Greek and Latin texts and religious tracts.[19] He was presented to the rectory of Ewhurst in Hampshire in 1659 by Oxford University, with the support of Richard Cromwell, but was ejected in 1661 and replaced from May 1661 to 1664 by

10   *Hist. Parl. Commons*, 1604–29, iii, 686–89.
11   Baigent and Millard, *Basingstoke*, 399–400; *Cal. SP Dom.* 1629–31, 533; K. Sharpe, *The Personal Rule of Charles I* (1992), 15.
12   HRO, 18M61/box C/bundle 4; box E/bundle 9.
13   Ibid., 18M61/box E/bundle 9.
14   Ibid., 71M82/PR1.
15   Ibid., 1616B/028.
16   Ibid., 1572B/005. The parish registers have survived from 1606 onwards and no Ayliffes are recorded.
17   See p. 85.
18   HRO, 18M61/box G/bundle 10. Crook sold to Mr William Nicholas of Barton Stacey the two yardlands in 1624 bundle 10, no. 6. The hearth tax for 1673–5 listed Mr John Orpwood in his freehold and in his parsonage house 12 but this is crossed out and the three for the parsonage left. In previous lists Orpwood is listed with three hearths, followed by Harmar with nine. After the deaths of the Harmars, Arthur Crook appeared to inhabit the house belonging to the freehold together with his one hearth copyhold. See TNA, E 179/176/570, June 1673 to March 1675. By 1703 Orpwood was the owner but there is a gap in the records from 1675–1703.
19   *ODNB* s.v., 'Harmar, John (1593x6–1670), Church of England clergyman and Greek scholar' (accessed 19 Oct. 2015).

John Orpwood, who held Ewhurst in plurality with Steventon for three years.[20] Social
relationships may have been a bit tense in Steventon with a learned Parliamentarian
cleric in close proximity to Sir John Lewknor, the Royalist lord of the manor, whose
estates at West Dean were sequestered in 1646 until he paid a fine of £1,440 for fighting
against Parliament.[21] Both John and Joanne Harmar died in 1670 with Joanne's inventory
valued at £125.[22]

In the absence of the lord of the manor, the leaseholder of the Manor farm and the
copyholders and freeholder led village society. John Brothers in 1648 leased Manor farm
comprising a four-hearth farmhouse, a messuage, a barn, an orchard and 30 a. of land for
three lives at an annual rent of £2 and a fine of £350.[23] Thomas Small (d. 1687) was the
wealthiest copyholder with five hearths. He paid an annual rent of £3 for a total of three
yardlands (c.90 a.) and some closes in Steventon. Small also held land in Basingstoke
leased for £48 a year and valued at £1,000. His servant's chamber had one bed. Attached
to his house were a mealhouse, a brewhouse, a milkhouse and stable.[24] Arthur Crook was
copyholder of 60 a. of land and had recently built a house, as instructed by his father,
with one hearth on this land before his family sold its 60 a. freehold in 1623–4.[25] By 1673
after the deaths of the Harmars, he appears to have returned to the freehold house, once
owned by his family, as a tenant.[26] A further four copyholders, William Passion,[27] Michael
Noyse, Charles Covey and Austin Ansell, held 30 a. of land each and had houses with one
or two hearths.[28] One copyholder had a cottage and 5 a. The other two who paid the tax
lived in one-hearth houses. The three non-chargeable households were cottagers.[29]

Social Structure c.1740–c.1980

In the 18th century, in the continued absence of a resident lord, parish society was
increasingly dominated by the tenant of the Manor farm and the rector. John Brothers
was succeeded by two William Parkers (father and son) and then Mr Hellier[30] as the
tenant of Manor farm.[31] The Parkers were tenants for the first 40 years of the 18th
century and took responsibility for church maintenance on behalf of the parish. William
Parker (d. 1718) was a wealthy man who left bequests of £800 to his younger son and
his two unmarried daughters.[32] This trend was accentuated when the lord of the manor
purchased the independent 60 a. freehold in 1736 which the Orpwoods had sold in

20 *Calamy Revised*, 248; HRO, 35M48/5/1.
21 *VCH Sussex*, IV (1953), 7; *Cal. SP Dom.* 1645–7, 588–9; *Cal. of the Cttee for Compounding* 1643–60, part
    2, 1215–17.
22 HRO, 71M82/PR1; 1670AD/122.
23 Ibid., 18M61/box E/ bundle 9.
24 Ibid., 1687AD/77.
25 Ibid., 18M61/box G/bundle 10; 1616B/028.
26 TNA, E 179/176/570 1673.
27 Variations of this name were Patience and Passiant.
28 HRO, 18M61/box C/bundle 4.
29 TNA, E 179/176/565, published as *Hearth Tax*, 427.
30 Variations of this name were Hellear and Hellyer.
31 HRO, 18M61/tin box C.
32 Ibid., 1718A/56.

Figure 18 *Digweed family memorial in St Nicholas church.*

1712.[33] From the 1760s the dominance of the chief tenant and rector became even more marked: the Digweeds were tenants of the Manor farm from 1765 to 1877, when their final lease and the immediate family expired. Between 1759 and 1855 the lords of the manor and the rectors were always related, enhancing the status of the rectors.

The social structure of local society is evident in Jane Austen's *Letters*.[34] The earls of Portsmouth, the dukes of Bolton and Lord Dorchester, three neighbouring peers, dominated north Hampshire society. The marginal social status of the clergy on the edge of gentry society is well portrayed. George Austen was related to Thomas Knight. George's uncle, Francis Austen, purchased the livings of Deane to increase George's income, which George also supplemented by teaching and farming, but even so this rector of Steventon still lacked the means to emulate the local gentry.[35] Steventon rectory was quite large but rather shabby and unimposing, three storeys high with kitchen gardens, farmyard and a long grassy bank, which in 1800 was partly planted with beech, ash, lime, thorns and lilac.[36] It had four sitting rooms, the contents of which were valued at £200 in 1801.[37] The relatively small size of the rectory meant that accommodating Christmas visitors for theatricals was a tight squeeze.[38] The Austens could afford some luxuries: Jane had a piano and decorative tables were purchased.[39] George's wife, Cassandra, inherited £1,000 from her mother which was invested in order to pay her £100 a year in widowhood.[40] The family had their own carriage in 1797–8, after which they decided it was too expensive.[41]

33   HRO, 18M61/box G/bundle 10.
34   Only 33 of the 161 published letters date from the years when Jane Austen lived at Steventon. The letters began in January 1796 when Jane Austen was 20 years old. The last one written from Steventon was dated Sunday 25 Jan. 1801.
35   *Family Record*, 6, 96. Numbers of pupils were reduced 1791–6 before he discontinued teaching.
36   Austen, *Letters*, 51.
37   Ibid., 72.
38   *Austen Papers*, 127–8.
39   *Reading Mercury*, notices of auctions, 4 May 1801, 14 Sept. 1801.
40   *Family Record*, 19.
41   Ibid., 96; Austen, *Letters,* 20 (Nov. 1798).

George Austen employed servants to wash for his household, to work in the dairy and to cook. Several members of the Littleworth family were servants to the Austens. Cassandra Austen, his wife, sent her infants to be cared for by nurses in the area.[42] The Austens were not wealthy and Jane reworked her dresses and hats.[43] Despite these limitations, the rector and the Digweeds were the prominent people of the parish in the absence of the lord of the manor.

There is little insight into the social status of the villagers of Steventon in the *Letters* except as servants to the Austen household or as the poor in receipt of charity.[44] The people described as neighbours by Jane Austen were the Bramstons of Oakley Hall and the Harwoods of Deane House or the Digweeds, the only family in Steventon with whom the Austens socialized.[45] Jane Austen was concerned about the fate of her father's bailiff at Cheesedown farm, John Bond, when Mr Holder took over the lease in 1801.[46] She also wrote warmly of Nanny Littleworth, with whom the young Austens were boarded as babies and for one of whose children she later became godmother.[47] However, Jane Austen was less charitable about Mrs Steevens who washed for the Austen household writing that 'she does not look as if anything she touched would ever be clean'.[48]

George Austen was succeeded as rector by his sons, James (1805–19), Henry (1820–3) and his grandson, William Knight, son of Edward Austen/Knight who had inherited the manor from his adopted father, Thomas Knight. The Revd William Knight belonged to the gentry and his lifestyle may be contrasted with the earlier Austens. Edward Knight commissioned a new rectory for William in 1823–4.[49] It was built on the hill opposite the old rectory but well above the damp valley in which the old rectory had been built. It was approached by a carriage drive and had beautiful views of the surrounding country. It was a gentleman's residence (Fig. 22) with five bedrooms, two dressing rooms, day and night nurseries, excellent dining and drawing rooms, library, considerable servants' accommodation, double coach-house and stabling for six horses, ornamental lawn and park.[50] Some 53 a. of glebe was attached to it and 46 a. of freehold land. William Knight paid a nominal rent of 5s. a year for the freehold land.[51] The glebe enhanced the social status of the rector, as did the new rectory. William Knight became a Justice of the Peace in 1839.[52]

When Edward Knight sold his estate in Steventon to the second duke of Wellington in 1855, the social status of William Francis Digweed was unchanged: he continued to lease the Manor House with four main bedrooms, drawing and dining rooms, lawn and pleasure gardens and views over the countryside, for which he paid £625 a year until his death in 1863.[53] In 1861 he employed five indoor servants under a housekeeper. In 1871

42   Austen, *Letters*, 18, 25; *Austen Papers, 28.*
43   Austen, *Letters*, 26, 30.
44   See p. 70.
45   Austen, *Letters*, 49.
46   Ibid., 73.
47   Ibid., 22; D. Le Faye, 'The Austens and the Littleworths', *Jane Austen Society Report* (1987), 15–21.
48   Austen, *Letters*, 18.
49   HRO, 18M61/box F/bundle 6.
50   Ibid., 68M72/DDZ14.
51   Ibid., 18M61/Map 28; 39M89/E/B76.
52   Ibid., Q27/3/389.
53   Ibid., 10M57/SP639.

John Digweed, a bachelor, aged 64, had inherited his uncle's lease as tenant of Manor farm, where he employed five domestic servants and four live-in farm servants. At the large and handsome rectory, the Revd William Knight employed six domestic servants including a ladies' maid, a cook, a coachman and a footman.[54] Digweed had a groom and a housekeeper. By 1867 the duke of Wellington had sold the advowson of the rectory and the lordship of the manor but not the land to the Revd Gilbert Alder.[55]

In 1877 the duke of Wellington sold the manor to Henry Harris, a corn factor, who intended to live in the parish and decided to replace the old Elizabethan manor house with a new Victorian mansion.[56] In 1891 Harris resided in the parish in his new mansion house (Fig. 14). He dominated social life and employed 12 domestic servants including a butler, parlour maid, three house maids, a cook, a kitchen maid, a scullery maid and three grooms. On a smaller scale, the rector, Revd Edward Alder, employed a governess and three domestic servants and had personal possessions worth £1,000 including household linen, printed books, wearing apparel, plate, watches, clocks, trinkets, wines, liquors, mathematical and musical instruments, china, glass, looking glasses, pictures and prints.[57] By April 1901 these leading men of the parish had died and their widows, Janet Harris and Naomi Alder, employed ten and three servants respectively. In 1901 Naomi Alder, widow of the Revd Edward Alder (d. Jan. 1901), sold the lordship of the manor to Henry Harris, son of the previous owner, who was thus able to unite the lordship of the manor with ownership of its land.[58] In 1910 the manor was sold to Mr Robert Henry Davis Mills, who in 1911 employed eight domestic servants. Mills was appointed Sheriff of the county of Southampton on 13 March 1917.[59] His successors, the Onslow Fanes (1926–39) and the Hutton Crofts (1936–67) continued to dominate local society until the Second World War, when the manor house was requisitioned and never again inhabited by the lords of the manor.

From 1851 to 1911 one or two villagers enhanced their social status by employing a servant. Mary Hutt, a grocer employed two in 1851 and Dennis Taylor, farmer of Cheesedown, employed one. In 1861 the shoemaker and the blacksmith each employed one servant. In 1871 the farm bailiff employed one as did the farm steward in 1881. In 1891, a carter, the blacksmith and one farmer each employed one and John Fooks, farmer, employed two, reduced to one by 1901. In 1911 a farmer employed one, and a platelayer employed a housekeeper.[60] Only 8 per cent of the servants employed by the rector, farmers and tradesmen of Steventon were born in the parish from 1851 to 1901, while 75 per cent originated from the surrounding parishes of north Hampshire and the remainder came from further afield.[61] In 1851 there was very limited population mobility with 52 per cent of the inhabitants born in Steventon and 37 percent in the surrounding parishes.[62] Ten per cent came from other southern counties. This had

54   Census 1861; *White's Dir. Hants. & IOW* (1859), 514; HRO, 5M62/6/489.
55   *Kelly's Dir. Hants.* (1867), 672.
56   *Post Office Dir. Hants.* (1875), 224. Census 1851–1911.
57   HRO, 49M84/C27/1/5.
58   Ibid., 23M71/LB1, 90; 46M84/C27/2/1; *Kelly's Dir. Hants.* (1903), 548.
59   HRO, Q21/2/86.
60   Census 1851–1911.
61   Census 1851–1911.
62   Census 1851.

changed significantly by 1901 with only 19 per cent born in Steventon, 45 per cent from Hampshire, 27 per cent from southern counties and a few from the Midlands and London. For example, the new owner of Cheesedown Farm, John Fooks, had moved from Dorset with his wife and three older children.[63] By 1926 population mobility had increased with the headmistress recording that in the last few years the population had become very transient.[64]

The Life of the Community

The Importance of Steventon in the Literary Career of Jane Austen

Jane Austen lived in Steventon from 1775 to 1800. These were the formative years of her career and have been described as the 'cradle of her genius'.[65] Her father encouraged her writing and she valued the role of the clergy in society. The Steventon parsonage was demolished soon after Austen's death, so it is only in St Nicholas church that her memory is commemorated.[66] Jane Austen spent her first 25 years at her father's parsonage in Steventon, where she was educated and informed by reading in her father's large library. On his retirement this contained 500 volumes including historical studies and the romantic and moral novels of Samuel Richardson (published 1740–53). George Austen encouraged Jane to read novels, including those by Samuel Richardson; the plays of Shakespeare; poems and histories, such as Robert Henry's *History of England* (six quarto volumes, 1771–93).[67] These genres were critical in her formative years when she had no personal contact with other authors. Jane Austen also collected her own books.[68] She analysed writing styles, plots and characters and gained ideas for settings and background.[69] Deirdre Le Faye suggested that Jane gained her intellect from her father and wit and acute observation of character from her mother.[70] The Austens loved drama. Theatricals were performed in the dining room at Steventon from 1782 or in her father's barn which by 1787 was fitted out as a theatre.[71] Large sets were painted as scenery.[72] Such performances were popular entertainment among fashionable and gentry families of the time[73] and taken very seriously by the Austens, their neighbours, the young Digweeds; and guests, such as Jane's cousins, Eliza de Feuillide and Philadelphia Walter. Parts were allocated well in advance and participants had to rehearse and wear appropriate costumes.[74] Jane's elder brother, James, wrote a prologue and epilogue in verse to *Matilda* by Sir Thomas Francklin. It was in this literary environment that Jane began writing short pieces, many of which were acted out by family and friends. She copied them into

63   Census 1901.
64   See pp. 68–9.
65   Austen-Leigh, *Memoir*, 22.
66   A bronze plaque in the north wall of the nave is dedicated to Jane Austen.
67   Austen, *Letters*, 59, 74.
68   Ibid., 77.
69   See for example, *Letters*, 22.
70   *Family Record*, 19.
71   Ibid., 46.
72   *Austen Papers*, 126.
73   See for example, A. Hare, *The Georgian Theatre in Wessex* (1958), 120–40.
74   *Austen Papers*, 126–8.

three notebooks now known as *Juvenilia* (1787–93). Much later these family theatricals inspired and lent authority to the theatricals in *Mansfield Park*.[75] Theatricals peaked for the Austen family in 1788 with performances every few months and finished in 1789 as James developed other interests.[76]

Jane Austen's novels drew on characters and manners she observed in local society.[77] Outside the parsonage, Jane Austen mixed with local families and gentry whom she observed acutely, drawing inspiration for the characters and sentiments portrayed in her writing. Her father also taught boarders, up to four sons of the gentry at any one time,[78] and prepared them for university, so Jane had considerable opportunity to observe the characteristics of young men both in these students and in her brothers. Jane benefited greatly from the conversation of parents, siblings and pupils in the rural parsonage of Steventon.[79] She became very aware of aristocratic pride and condescension and the limitations imposed by society on those of limited means.[80] In 1783 the Lefroy family moved into Ashe parsonage and Mrs Lefroy, a poetry lover, provided Jane Austen with intellectual stimulus.[81] Jane Austen was saddened when romance did not flourish between her and Tom Lefroy, a visitor to Ashe, but the feelings she experienced and tears shed enabled her to portray the emotional sufferings of her heroines realistically.[82] Austen also understood the impact on her own marriage prospects of having no dowry.

Her powers of observation and social contacts enabled her to create distinctive characters with realistic and appealing or repelling qualities. She developed the skill of caricature and endowed her fictional characters with peculiarities and weaknesses which made them realistic.[83] Jane Austen also became very aware of family tensions, the inequalities of society and the interaction between aristocracy, gentry and the clergy. She socialized in north Hampshire society. Jane also visited her brother, Edward, at Rowling, and after 1798, at Godmersham in Kent, which gave her personal insight into life in great houses. Such experience was essential for a female writer of the time who was expected to write from her own experience. Letters received from her brothers, Frank and Charles, both naval officers, gave her an understanding of the impact of war.[84] Jane Austen also gained some insight into farming as her father was tenant of Cheesedown farm.[85] The rural scene apparently encouraged Jane Austen to write and her career began in Steventon, paused in Bath and Southampton and resumed once she settled in Chawton from July 1809.[86] In 1797 George Austen first approached a London publisher, Mr Cadell, on his daughter's behalf but with no success. From January 1799 Jane enjoyed novels and other literature from Mrs Martin's subscriber library.[87] However, this was later much

75   Austen-Leigh, *Memoir*, 25.
76   *Family Record*, 64. B. Southam, 'Juvenilia', in J. David Grey (ed.), *The Jane Austen Handbook* (1986), 248.
77   Austen, *Letters*, x, 52–3.
78   Collins, *Parson's Daughter*, 16.
79   Ibid., 61. The parsonage was demolished *c*.1824.
80   Austen, *Letters*, passim; Collins, *Parson's Daughter*, 59, 227.
81   *Family Record*, 44; Collins, *Parson's Daughter*, 95–6.
82   Austen, *Letters*, 4, 19.
83   See for example, Austen, *Letters*, 61.
84   Collins, *Parson's Daughter*, 133. See for example, Austen, *Letters*, 32, 36, 52.
85   Ibid., 24.
86   Austen, *Letters*, 178 and 401, n. 2.
87   Austen, *Letters*, 26.

surpassed in her opinion by the book society in Chawton in 1813 which other societies emulated.[88]

The first versions of three of her most famous novels were written at Steventon. *Pride and Prejudice* (1813) was written between October 1796 and August 1797 with the title *First Impressions*.[89] *Elinor and Marianne*, the early version of *Sense and Sensibility* (1811) followed, reflecting contrasting contemporary views on the importance of sentiment. *Northanger Abbey* (1818) was first written as *Susan* in 1798. These novels were written on the writing desk purchased for Jane Austen in 1794 by her father, from John Ring of Basingstoke (Fig. 19).[90]

Social Life from the Letters

Jane Austen's *Letters* also offer a unique insight into the opportunities for, and limitations of, social life for the gentry both in Steventon and north Hampshire at the end of the 18th century. Jane Austen liked dancing and attended assembly balls at Basingstoke and private balls in the area surrounding Basingstoke in winter 1798–9. She recorded the decline of the assemblies in Basingstoke until, in November 1798, only 27 people attended, with just seven couples dancing.[91] In January 1799 she lamented that the ball was a poor one with only eight couples and just 23 people in the room, of whom most were Jervoises from Herriard, and Terrys from Dummer. She reflected that the Jervoises were 'apt to be vulgar' and the Terrys were noisy.[92] In 1798–9 Austen enjoyed private balls at Hurstbourne Park, the home of the earl of Portsmouth; at Hackwood House, the seat of the dukes of Bolton; at Manydown in Wootton St Lawrence, the home of the Bigg-Withers, and at Kempshott Park, where the tenant was Lord Dorchester.[93] Lord Portsmouth's ball at Hurstbourne Park in November 1800 attracted 50 guests. As a child, the future earl had been a pupil of George Austen and lived at Steventon rectory briefly before Jane was born.[94] The previous month, Jane Austen observed the hierarchy of local society reflecting that the 60 present at a ball were made up of Portsmouths, Dorchesters, Boltons, Portals and Clerks and 'all the meaner and more usual, etc'.[95]

Visiting was an important part of Jane Austen's social life in Steventon. She frequently went on foot, an experience later reflected in her novels, to visit neighbours such as the Harwoods in Deane House, the Portals in Ashe, the Bramstons in Oakley Hall and Mrs Lefroy, wife of the rector of Ashe.[96] Similarly the Austens received visitors such as Mrs Heathcote of Hursley Park, Mrs Harwood, Mrs James Austen, the Misses Bigg[97] of Manydown Park, Miss Jane Blachford, of Osborne House, Isle of Wight, but a frequent visitor at Manydown Park, and Mr James Holder, tenant of the Portals, at Ashe Park.[98]

88   Austen, *Letters*, 199.
89   *Family Record*, 94–5.
90   HRO, 8M62/15.
91   Austen, *Letters*, 20, 22; 68.
92   Ibid., 38.
93   Ibid., 25, 28–9, 32, 33, 605.
94   Ibid., 60 and 371, n. 2.
95   Austen, *Letters*, 53.
96   Ibid., 9, 49, 80.
97   Elizabeth, Catherine and Alethea Bigg were friends of Jane Austen (Austen, *Letters*, 497).
98   Austen, *Letters*, 72, 6.

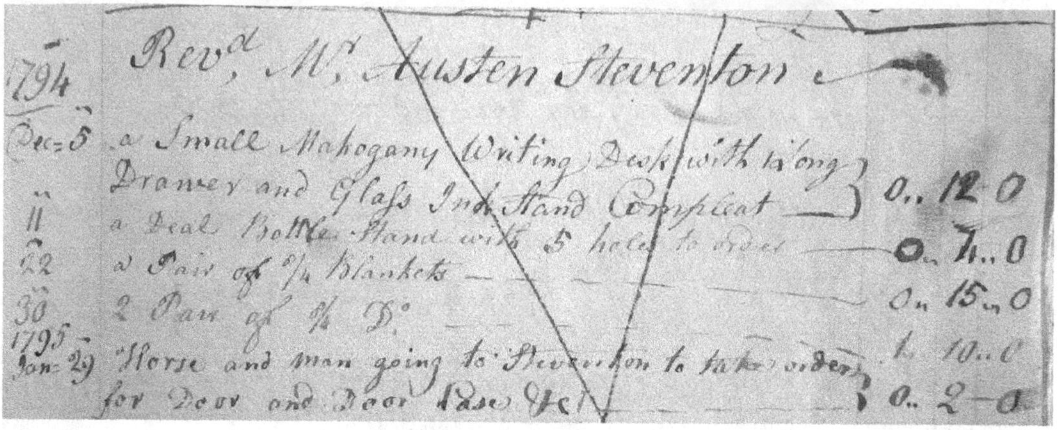
1794 Revd. Mr. Austen Steventon
Dec 5 a Small Mahogany Writing Desk with 1 long Drawer and Glass Ink Stand Compleat 0..12..0
11 a Deal Bottle Stand with 5 holes to order 0..7..0
22 a Pair of 9/4 Blankets 0..15..0
30 2 Pair of 9/4 Do 1..10..0
1795 Jan 29 Horse and man going to Steventon to take orders for Door and Door Case &c 0..2..0

Figure 19 *Extract from John Ring's sales book, 1792–6.*

Close neighbours dined at the rectory, such as the Digweeds and her brother, James, but they were limited in number and Austen noted how dinner parties with the same people present could be tedious.[99]

From early 1801 Jane, her sister, Cassandra, and her parents moved to Bath on her father's retirement, leaving her brother, James, as curate of Steventon.[100] Experience of Bath assemblies later confirmed Jane's view of the inferiority of Basingstoke. She wrote on 12 May 1801 there were enough people at a 'shockingly and inhumanly thin for this place' (Bath) to make five to six very pretty Basingstoke assemblies.[101]

Gentry Sport 1700–2015

In 1363 Bernard Brocas had been granted free warren.[102] In 1741 the lord of the manor, Thomas Knight, when leasing his land, reserved the woods to himself with the right to hunt and shoot. By 1806 this was extended to 'hunting, shooting, coursing, fishing, sporting'.[103] In 1743 Knight enquired whether the duke of Bolton's estate at Hackwood Park could supply any deer.[104] The chief tenants of the Knights enjoyed sporting rights: in 1798 Harry Digweed, tenant of Steventon Manor, purchased the right to shoot game from Edward Austen.[105] In 1812 it was reported that 'Mr Digweed is going on Tuesday to Steventon to shoot rabbits'.[106] In 1855 the estate was described as 'admirably adapted for any gentleman fond of sporting' with partridges, hares and pheasants nurtured on the lands and woods.[107] In 1851 Charles Littleworth was gamekeeper, the first mention of an occupation which grew in importance by the end of the 19th century.[108] From 1861

99 Austen, *Letters*, 31, 75–6, 78.
100 *ODNB* s.v., 'Austen, Jane (1775–1817) novelist' (accessed 11 Sept. 2011).
101 Austen, *Letters*, 85.
102 HRO, 18M61/E. K. 2/box 2/bundle 20; *Cal. Chart.* V, 1341–1417, 178.
103 HRO, 18M61/E. K. 2/box 2/bundle 20.
104 Ibid., 18M61/tin box C.
105 Austen, *Letters*, 15, 18.
106 Ibid., 196.
107 HRO, 10M57/SP639.
108 Census, 1851.

to 1881 no gamekeepers are recorded but in 1891 and 1901 there were three living in Warren Keepers cottages. In 1911 two lived in the Warren cottages and one at Misholt.[109]

In 1910 there were 227 a. of woods belonging to the manor reserved for shooting, especially of partridge and pheasant.[110] By 1926, 213 a. for shooting were rented out at £550 a year. Steventon Manor was described as a fine sporting and residential estate which claimed to have 'one of the best shoots in Hampshire' with proximity to the Vyne and Hampshire packs of foxhounds for hunting.[111] In 1926 1,000 pheasants' eggs were put down for the next season. There were also 57 a. of rabbit warrens and rough land. Game bags included pheasants, partridges, hares and rabbits. A Thornycroft lorry 'was fitted with special seating to carry the 'guns' on shooting days'. The gamekeeper had three assistants to look after the pheasants, partridges and hares. [112]

Community Activities and Public Buildings

Steventon families enjoyed the annual fair at Basingstoke with, for example, 13 children missing school to attend in October 1897.[113] The Band of Hope organized summer picnics for the children of the parish.[114] A Boy Scout group was active in the village by 1912.[115]

Parish social meetings took place in the school from 1895, until a church room (Fig. 20) was erected in 1932, which provided a focus for village social life.[116] French doors in the south wall opened onto a lawn. A small room served as a kitchen.[117] The village children gave concerts in the glebe barn during the First World War to raise money for the League of Young Patriots' fund and for blind soldiers.[118] The lord of the manor provided entertainments for the villagers: for example, the school was closed for a half day in January 1936 so the children could attend the parish tea given by Mr Jack Onslow Fane.[119] There were extensive celebrations in 1975, including play-readings in the Victorian stable block, for the 200th anniversary of Jane Austen's birth.[120] Some of the money raised was spent on improving the church room which was renamed Steventon Village Hall in 1979 and was used for harvest festival suppers, whist drives, Christmas bazaars and private hire by residents. At the beginning of the 21st century a pantomime was staged in February of each year.

109 Census 1861–1911.
110 HRO, 62A00/1.
111 Ibid., 46M84/F86/3.
112 Ibid., 46M84/F86/3.
113 Ibid., 23M71/LB1, 46.
114 See for example, HRO, 23M71/LB1, 234.
115 Ibid., 23M71/LB1, 298.
116 *Kelly's Dir. Hants.* (1939), 540.
117 LPL, ECE/7/1/84906.
118 HRO, 23M71/LB1, 353, 380.
119 Ibid., 71M82/PJ1, 25.
120 Le Faye, *Steventon*, 16.

Figure 20 *The Village Hall (originally the Church Room) in 2014.*

Women's Institute

Steventon Women's Institute (WI) was formed on 28 November 1917 with 17 members who met monthly.[121] Mrs Mills, wife of the lord of the manor, was president, with the rector's wife, Mrs Steedman, as vice-president. The school mistress, Miss A. E. Taylor, was secretary. Initially they met in the school but a hut was acquired in the 1920s. Meetings were described as friendly and included flower growing and arranging and sweet-making competitions, with talks for example on bandaging or lantern-making.[122]

By the mid 1930s the WI was struggling and dissension was apparent from 1932 when the annual inspection by the Hampshire Federation of WIs lamented the failure of new members to observe the rules. There was open discord by 1937 when it was proposed to suspend meetings for a year. Hampshire Federation visited in July 1937 and found only two members present: no programme arranged and no subscriptions paid.[123] In the same year, the hut was sold for £25 and the money invested to hire the newly constructed church hall for meetings. There was distrust of the treasurer by other members. Some members wanted to merge with North Waltham WI but others, including the vice president were opposed. One member said the days of WIs were ended, another that villagers thought WIs were for 'chapel folk'. The Federation representative accepted the

---

121 The WI text is based on HRO, 96M96/99/2 unless otherwise stated.

122 HRO, 96M96/99/2.

123 Ibid.

suspension of the meeting, and took the books and money in hand, noting 'all three officers so-called ... seem to have been more than unkind.'[124]

Steventon WI was revived in 1963 with 20 members attending monthly meetings in the Church Room. Meetings included talks, refreshments, games and competitions.[125] An annual May fair and excursions to the theatre in London and Portsmouth added variety. The WI met for four more years until summer 1967 when enthusiasm waned. At the AGM in December no one was prepared to serve as an officer. The last meeting was held in January 1968 with ten members and a Federation representative. The WI was suspended and finally shut down in March 1971, selling its crockery to North Waltham WI for £5.[126]

Education

Education before 1870

By 1808 and probably earlier, Edward Austen paid £5 a year to his chief tenant, W. F. Digweed, for a school for the poor in Steventon. In 1819 there was a school for about ten children which met the needs of the poor of the parish.[127] There is no indication of where the school was held but it taught five girls and six boys in 1821 and six boys and 15 girls in 1831.[128] By 1845 the annual payment for the schoolmistress, paid by the Revd William Knight on behalf of his father, had risen to £8.[129] In 1859 Elizabeth Green was the school mistress.[130] The duke of Wellington supported the school from 1855 to 1877.[131] By 1880 Henry Harris paid £10 a year to maintain this school, described as a dame school, at which 15–20 children were taught in a dwelling room of a very poor cottage in which an 'extremely old woman occupies an armchair by the fire', the books and apparatus being apparently a lidless box on the floor full of detached sheets of reading primers.[132] The rector, Revd Herbert Alder, responded that the teacher, Mrs Myrtle, was 61 with 18 children on the register.[133] There was also a Sunday School with 13 attending in 1821 and 21 in 1831.[134]

After 1870

An assessment following Forster's Education Act of 1870, which stated that elementary education should be provided for all children, identified 35 Steventon children who needed educational provision.[135] The older children from the parish went to North

124 HRO, 96M96/99/2.
125 Ibid., 96M96/99/1.
126 Ibid., 96M96/99/2.
127 *Parl. Papers*, Digest of Parochial Returns on Schools, 1819 (224).
128 HRO, 79M78/B211, 21M65/B5/2.
129 Ibid., 79M78/B212.
130 *White's Dir. Hants. & IOW* (1859), 514.
131 *Post Office Dir. Hants.* (1867), 672.
132 TNA, ED 2/204.
133 Ibid.
134 HRO, 21M65/B5/2.
135 TNA, ED 2/204.

Waltham school, while infants were still taught by Mrs Harriett Myrtle.[136] A campaign for a school in Steventon was led by Henry Harris as North Waltham school was too far away for children to walk. The L&SWR, the biggest rate-payer in Steventon, was asked to contribute to the cost of building a school but refused. Harris declined to finance it all himself and no other parishioners could afford to pay. As a result of the local campaign, the Education Department in London was forced, very reluctantly, in September 1893 to set up a school board for Steventon and to build a school to accommodate all 60 of the Steventon children assessed as needing state education.[137] On 12 February 1894 plans were exhibited for a brick built school with a tiled roof, comprising two school rooms: one 25ft x 18ft for older pupils and another 14ft x 18ft for the infants (Fig. 21). A six-room house for the schoolmistress was to be built next door. The total cost was £1,250.[138] The school opened on 8 October 1894 with 43 pupils. In 1904 the main school room had floor space for 45 while the infants' room had space for 27, though attendance was 25 and 15 respectively. Numbers remained fairly constant with 44 pupils attending in 1903.[139] The three-bedroom teacher's house was detached from the school but on the same site. Drinking water was supplied from a well in the teacher's garden to both school and house, but in 1904 the drains of both needed some work.[140]

The school was visited by Henry Harris and the rector, the Revd Edward Alder.[141] HMI's reports of the school were generally satisfactory with indoor and outdoor sports taught alongside more academic subjects and an increase of numbers in 1905 to 51 but the school mistress changed frequently.[142] By October 1907 when Mrs Daisy Tod was the schoolmistress and Mrs Ida Weeks was the infants' mistress, the numbers of pupils had fallen to 41 as many families had left the village.[143] The Revd and Mrs Steedman and Mrs Harris were frequent visitors to the school from 1908: they listened to the children reading and singing and presented prizes for good work.[144] There were criticisms of both the standard of teaching and the lack of cleanliness in the school. The frequent job moves of agricultural labourers and resulting lack of stability in the school population were blamed for falling standards of the children who were described by the inspector, J. Hodges, as part of a 'migratory backward class'.[145]

From 1917, pupils cultivated gardens of the several empty cottages to aid the war effort.[146] This ceased after the war to the disappointment of the inspector, Miss G. M. Stone, who thought practical classes of some kind would be of great value to these children 'to whom the formal side of school work must seem to have little connection with their experiences outside'.[147] In 1926 the headmaster resigned and noted that in the last three years 72 children had been admitted, but of these only 30 remained in

136 *White's Dir. Hants.* (1878), 582.
137 TNA, ED 2/204.
138 Ibid., ED 21/6593.
139 *Kelly's Dir. Hants.* (1898), 520; 1903, 548.
140 HRO, 48M71/28, 60.
141 Ibid., 23M71/LB1, 1–2.
142 Ibid., 23M71/LB1, 201.
143 Ibid., 23M71/LB1, 226. *Kelly's Dir. Hants.* (1907), 557.
144 HRO, 23M71/LB1, 228–62, passim.
145 Ibid., 23M71/LB1, 272.
146 Ibid., 23M71/LB1, 364–5. Three empty cottages were listed in the 1911 census.
147 HRO, 23M71/LB1, 416–7.

Figure 21 *The Old Steventon School in 2014.*

the school. During the previous year 28 children had left and 26 children had been admitted.[148] This trend continued in 1929 when children, who had not been well taught, had moved into the village. Some pupils spoke very badly and needed to improve their 'slovenly articulation' before they left school.[149] Reports then improved and in 1935 the school was described as hardworking.[150] From 1938 the Church Room was used for short domestic science courses.[151] In February 1941, 30 pupils from the village attended the school and 19 evacuees, giving a total on the roll of 49. Of these, 42 were under 11s and seven were seniors.[152]

In 1945 there were 35 pupils. Electric lighting was installed in 1946.[153] The school was no longer considered adequate for the pupils aged over 11, who in 1949 were transferred to Whitchurch secondary modern school.[154] Such assessments occurred throughout England as a result of Butler's Education Act, 1944.[155] Steventon school reopened in September 1949 as a junior school with an average attendance of 19.[156] Mrs G. Tanner

148 HRO, 23M71/LB1, 487.
149 Ibid., 23M71/LB2, 15–7.
150 TNA, ED 21/29576.
151 Ibid., ED 21/52420; HRO, 71M82/PJ1, 43.
152 Ibid., 23M71/LB2, 121.
153 HRO, 71M82/PJ1.
154 TNA, ED 161/6352.
155 7 & 8 Geo 6 c.31.
156 HRO, 23M71/LB2, 184.

was a successful headmistress from 1940 to 1964, praised in 1963 for her long and devoted service and the good written and oral standards attained by her pupils. On her retirement, Hampshire Education Committee decided to close Steventon school and send its pupils to North Waltham. Junior pupils transferred in April 1964, with the infants following in September after the summer holidays. Steventon school finally closed on 29 July 1964 and became a private house (Fig. 21).[157] In 2014 there was a Montessori nursery school in Steventon village hall on weekdays.[158]

Charity

Digweed's charity began in 1874 when William Henry Digweed bequeathed £100 to the rector and churchwardens of Steventon to invest for the benefit of the poor of the parish. It was registered with the Charity Commission in 1964. Small amounts were paid out each year with, for example, a total of £15 being given to the old people of the parish from 1952 to 1957.[159] In 2010 the charity was wound up with the permission of the Charity Commissioners as it had almost exhausted its funds.[160] What remained was transferred to the Parochial Church Council.

Poor Relief

None of the 14 surviving wills of Steventon residents in the 16th century made a bequest to the poor of the parish.[161] In the 17th century only four testators left bequests to the poor: Richard Perrin (d. 1626) left 2s. 6d. and Richard Woodruff (d. 1641) left 2s. to the poor of the parish and 10s. to the poorest sort of spinners who came to his house for work, to be divided amongst them at his funeral.[162] William Passion (d. 1676) and Elizabeth Smith (d. 1681) left 5s. and 10s. respectively to the poor.[163] In the 18th century the tenant of the Manor farm, William Parker (d. 1718) left £2 to the poor of the parish.[164]

Jane Austen gave clothes to poor villagers, probably paid for by her brother, Edward. In 1798 she gave a pair of worsted stockings to Mary Hutchins, Dame Kew, Mary Stevens, Dame Staples; a shift to Hannah Staples and a shawl to Betty Dawkins, which in total cost half a guinea.[165] In October 1800 Jane Austen purchased at Oakley ten pairs of worsted stockings and a shift for Betty Dawkins and commented that 'she is one of the most grateful of all whom Edward's charity has reached'.[166] Edward Knight was spending £5 a year on the poor of Steventon in 1845 but this charity had apparently been operating for a long time before then.[167]

157 TNA, ED 161/6352.
158 http://www.the-childrens-house.co.uk/steventon-childrens-house (accessed 14 Jan. 2014).
159 HRO, 71M82/PK1; CC no. 232705.
160 http://www.charitycommission.gov.uk/find-charities/accessed (accessed 14 Jan. 2014).
161 HRO, 1568B/043. John Fry (d. 1568) left 1 a. of barley to the poor of Kingsclere.
162 HRO, 1626A/94, 1641A/130.
163 Ibid., 1676A/76, 1681B/57.
164 Ibid., 1718A/56.
165 Austen, Letters, 31.
166 Ibid., 50.
167 HRO, 79M78/B212.

Very little is known about parish poor relief in Steventon as no accounts survive before 1907.[168] There was a parish poor house by 1743. It was not a workhouse but its exact use is not known.[169] In 1775–6 £18 was disbursed on out relief of the poor by the overseers.[170] In 1783–5, at the beginning of the French wars, the average yearly expenditure was £36. Following the national pattern, expenditure rose dramatically to £86 in 1802–3 after ten years of French wars when nine paupers received permanent out relief and 15 were relieved occasionally. Six children also received poor relief.[171] From 1806 the lord of the manor also granted a copyhold cottage to overseers of the poor for the use of the poor.[172] Expenditure rose rapidly in Steventon to a yearly average of £231 from 1816 to 1819 in the post-war slump.[173] During the 1820s expenditure was reduced to £100–£150 a year but it rose rapidly from 1829 to 1832 with an expenditure of £252 in 1831–2.[174] Steventon was a typical southern agricultural parish, where high costs of poor rates were a substantial burden. The Poor Law Amendment Act of 1834 attempted to reduce costs by proposing that relief should only be available in a workhouse.[175] Under this act, care of the poor in Steventon became the responsibility of the guardians of Basingstoke Poor Law Union, and the workhouse in Old Basing parish. Expenditure consequently fell dramatically, averaging £136 a year from 1835 to 1842.[176] This system continued until abolished by the Local Government Act of 1929.

Settlement and Bastardy

There is little surviving evidence of settlement issues in Steventon. Only three removal orders survive; one to the parish (1822) and two out of the parish (1797 and 1816).[177] One bastardy order survives from 1790.[178]

168 Overseers accounts only survive for the period 1907–27 held with the Basingstoke Poor Law Union Records, HRO, 68M72/DU41.
169 Ibid., 18M61/tin box C.
170 *Parl. Papers, 1776–7 Poor Abstract*, 453.
171 *Parl. Papers, 1803–4 (175). Poor Abstract*, 450. HRO, 16M79/2.
172 Ibid., 18M61/box G/bundle 6.
173 *Parl. Papers, 1822 (556) Poor Returns*.
174 *Parl. Papers 1830–31 (83) Poor Returns 1825–9, Parl. Papers, 1835 (444) Poor Returns 1830–4*.
175 See for example, K.D.M. Snell, *Parish and Belonging: Community, Identity and Welfare in England and Wales, 1700–1950* (2006).
176 *Parl. Papers 1837–38 (147) Poor Returns 1837–8; 1844 (63); Poor Returns 1839–42*.
177 HRO, 3M70/56/22; 19M76/PO5/731; 19M76/PO5/319. None of the parliamentary returns of 1777, 1803, 1829 record expenditure on litigation relating to settlement.
178 HRO, 44M69/G3/729.

LOCAL GOVERNMENT

Hundred Court of Basingstoke

UNTIL 1841, STEVENTON was in the hundred of Basingstoke,[1] to which the manor owed suit of court.[2] In the Middle Ages, the responsibility for the maintenance of peace was carried out through the community or tithings. All males over the age of 12 had to be enrolled and the chosen tithing man was responsible for reporting all infringements of the peace to the view of frankpledge court held twice a year in Basingstoke. Steventon, together with most of the other parishes in the hundred, made a payment of cert money to the court so it would operate as a frankpledge court, but Steventon's was the highest sum paid by any of the rural parishes.[3] The tithing men made their presentments to the courts recording offences against the peace, men who had failed to attend or be in the tithing, those who had brewed and broken the assizes of ale (usually one) and occasionally millers who had taken excessive toll, and issues concerning stray animals.[4] At the view of frankpledge held at Basingstoke in April 1399, the tithing man paid a 4s. instalment of cert money and presented John Levers, junior, John Pykamour, and Nicholas Burell as each had made two brewings of ale and broken the assize and were therefore at the mercy of the court. They were fined 6d. each.[5] Its role seems to have been reduced in the later 15th century. By the 16th century, it had ceased to act on offences concerning brewing, but continued to maintain the regulation of the tithing, paid certs and dealt with occasional stray sheep.[6] In 1561 the entire tithing of Steventon was ordered to provide stocks, fit for punishment of malefactors and vagabonds according to the statute before the feast of Pentecost next under penalty of 6s. 8d.[7] The tithingman was also responsible for responding to government queries about the resources of the parish in wartime, as in 1798 when he submitted the return of able–bodied men, cattle and crops to the hundred court.[8]

In 1261 the tithingman was criticized in the case of William le Niweman of Steventon who had had been arrested on suspicion of robbing the church of Steventon, of which he was subsequently found not guilty, but he escaped from prison in Basingstoke and for that was condemned to be hanged but the rope broke. It was alleged that he made

1   Youngs, *Admin. Units* I, 223. From 1841 Steventon was in Overton Hundred.
2   TNA, C 143/338/12; Baigent and Millard, *Basingstoke*, 307, 309, 329, 345, 239, 241, 289, 305, 343, 345.
3   Ibid., 239.
4   Ibid., 305; HRO, 148M71/2/7/1, 2/7/2, 2/1/1115, 2/1/34, 2/1/47, 2/1/52.
5   Baigent and Millard, *Basingstoke*, 305.
6   HRO, 148M71/68, 70, 71, 73.
7   Baigent and Millard, *Basingstoke*, 344.
8   HRO, Q22/1/2/5/10.

his escape by the fault of the bailiffs of Basingstoke and the tithingman of Steventon.[9] In the late 16th and early 17th century the lord of the manor, Sir Pexall Brocas, failed to maintain order. He imprisoned people who sought to complain about him at the Assizes and defrauded a family called Willson in Winchester. He was also indicted for the murder of Roger Knight who was found hanged in Haslingdown copse, Steventon, in 1607. The tithingman was responsible for calling in the coroner, George Scullard of Upper Clatford, and organized a jury of 20 to investigate the death. Scullard was satisfied that Knight had committed suicide and that the allegations arose from the hostility between Sir Pexall and Edward Savage.[10]

Manorial Courts 1600–1800

A court baron was held regularly to manage the manor's copyhold estates. Freeholders, leaseholders and copyholders owed homage to the court which was usually convened by the lord of the manor but occasionally by the steward. Absentee lords of the manor relied on their agent and chief tenant to manage the estate and negotiate tithes with the rector.[11] Records survive of the manorial courts of the lords of the manor from the early 17th century until the late 18th century.[12] Coteel held a court in Steventon in 1632 at which tenants surrendered their copies, frequently to secure a regrant for a different three lives, paying rents, fines and heriots at the appropriate times.[13] In 1729 all those with rights for stints of cattle on the commons and common fields were listed with their entitlements.[14] Transactions of c.1740 show that Thomas Knight, having recently inherited the estate, bought out the interests of his copyholders in land to facilitate the inclosure of the remaining open fields to create a new farm with those fields, the commons and other purchased land.[15] Later, in 1767, the Hellier family surrendered a messuage, garden and 4 a. on which a barn stood so that it could be regranted to the Revd George Austen, Cassandra, his wife, and James, his son. George paid an annual rent of 2s., a fine of £7 10s. and committed to the payment of a heriot.[16]

Parish Government and Officers

Churchwardens and overseers were clearly appointed in Steventon: overseers made returns to parliament; churchwardens were named in the episcopal visitations but overseers' accounts only survive from 1907 to 1927 and churchwardens' accounts from 1923 to 1948.[17] One church warden was appointed by the rector and one by the parishioners.[18]

9   *Cal. Inq. Misc.* I, 579 (2167), temp. Hen. III undated.
10   HRO, 49M69/G3/1124.
11   See for example, HRO, 18M61/tin box C.
12   HRO, 18M61/box C/bundle 4.
13   Ibid., 18M61/box C/bundle 4.
14   Ibid., 18M61/tin box C.
15   Ibid., 18M61/box 23.
16   Ibid., 18M61/tin box C.
17   Ibid., 68M72/DU41; 71M82/PW3.
18   Ibid., 71M82/PW3.

Steventon was created a civil parish coterminous with the then ecclesiastical parish under the Local Government Act (1894). It was part of Basingstoke Rural District Council from 1894 to 1974 and Henry Harris was the first councillor to represent Steventon on the new rural district council. Steventon, with a population of 249 in 1895, could have had a parish meeting rather than a parish council but the parish meeting chose to have a parish council. The county council order setting up the parish council and stating that five councillors should be elected was passed on 6 May 1895.[19] Parish councils were supposed to democratize local government but, as elsewhere, most of the new councillors were drawn from the local hierarchy. The first five councillors were the lord of the manor, Henry Harris; the rector, Edward Alder; John H. Fooks, farmer of Cheesedown; George Stone, Harris's bailiff; with only George Soper, a bootmaker, representing the ordinary people of the village.[20] Following local government reorganization in 1974, the parish became part of Basingstoke and Deane Borough Council. In 2015 the parish council still had five members who worked on local issues such as protecting footpaths, controlling hedges, planning issues and local road surfaces.[21]

19   HRO, W/A8/7, 91, 287–8.
20   *Hants. Chron.*, 26 March 1898; Census 1891.
21   Local inf. No records of the parish council meetings are in the public domain. http://steventonvillage.
co.uk/category/parish-council (accessed 27 Oct. 2015).

A FRAGMENT OF A cross (Fig. 5) discovered in the wall of the manor house suggests a Christian presence from about the late 8th or early 9th century. Steventon had its own church by c.1200, just to the east of the manor house. The living (a rectory) was well endowed in the medieval period but, at the end of the 16th century, the lord of the manor, who was patron of the living, seized the glebe and tithes. The tithes were restored with only a tiny fraction of the glebe; an additional 50 a. of glebe was added in the early 19th century and the church was restored and modernized from about the middle of that century onwards. The parish became part of a united benefice in 1930, after which the rectory house and glebe were sold. There was a Methodist chapel in the parish from 1903 to 1975.

Parochial Organization

Until 1930 the church was served by a rector, at times assisted by a curate. Steventon parish was united with North Waltham in 1930 despite a resolution by Steventon Parochial Church Council (PCC) that the merger would 'be detrimental to the spiritual welfare of the parish of Steventon'.[1] At the same time, a section of the ecclesiastical parish of Steventon north of the railway and including Cheesedown Farm was transferred from Steventon to Deane ecclesiastical parish.[2] In 1961 Steventon and North Waltham were united into one benefice with Dummer.[3] In 1972 a new benefice was created of North Waltham and Steventon, Ashe and Deane.[4] Steventon has been in the deanery of Basingstoke from the 16th century or earlier.[5]

Advowson

Between the 13th century and the 19th century, the patronage of the parish church belonged to the lord of the manor. In 1238, Hugh de Wengham and his wife and Philip de Sanderville, heirs of Geoffrey de Luverez, agreed to present the clerk in turns.[6] Occasionally an exception occurred as in 1396 when the king presented.[7] Exceptions also occurred in the 1590s and 1600s when, as a result of Sir Pexall Brocas's neglect of

1 HRO, 71M83/PW3; Order in council, *London Gaz.*, 23 March 1928.
2 LPL, ECE/7/1/84906; HRO, 66M83/PB6 (map).
3 *Crockford Clerical Dir.* (1963–4), 893.
4 HRO, 71M82/PB3; 45M84/4.
5 Ibid., 21M65/B1.
6 *VCH Hants.* IV, 174, citing TNA, CP 25/1/203/7/222.
7 *Reg. Wykeham*, I, f.202. Why this happened is unclear as Bernard Brocas had succeeded his father, also Bernard, in 1395 as patron of the living.

the church, the Crown presented in 1598 and the bishop of Winchester in 1602.[8] In the
mid 19th century, the advowson and the lordship of the manor were sold separately
from most of the land in the parish to the Revd Gilbert Alder whose family retained the
advowson until 1930.[9] In 1930 when North Waltham and Steventon parishes were united,
the Alder family sold the advowson to the Martyrs' Memorial Trust.[10] In 1947 the patrons
of the united living were the bishop of Winchester and the Martyrs' Memorial Trust
alternating.[11] From 1972 the bishop of Winchester alone was the patron of the enlarged
living.[12]

Glebe and Tithes

Glebe

The living was valued at £10 in 1291.[13] In 1341 the endowment of the church comprised
one messuage, one carucate of land (c.120 a.), a dovecote and rents to the value of 76s.
8d.[14] In 1512 the rectory was endowed with a glebe of 150 a., large for the size of the
parish, partly in closes and partly interspersed in the common fields, together with
grazing rights for 120 sheep, six cows, one bull and six horses.[15] During the next 100
years this glebe was seized by the lords of the manor and ultimately amalgamated with
the manorial estate. In 1544 Sir Richard Pexall had withheld from the parson, John
Bennett, and his lessee, John Cooke, the land, oblations and tithes, of his manor and farm
of Steventon for six years, depriving Cooke of an estimated £42–£48 in total. Pexall had
also inclosed 300 a. of the Southdown, thereby depriving the parson and his lessee of
common rights for 12 cows, one bull, six horses, 12 hogs, and one boar. Pexall had also
inclosed some of the glebe called Parson's Hassock. John Cooke obtained a Chancery
decree instructing Pexall to break down his inclosure and restore the Southdown to the
parsonage and the poor of Steventon and to pay Cook £20 arrears of tithe and £5 for his
costs in bringing the suit.[16] A generation later, however, in 1591–2 Pexall's grandson, Sir
Pexall Brocas, was instructed by the Privy Council to return rents and tithes to the widow
of the late rector of Steventon, Dr Ralph Thomason, or to appear before the Council.[17]
Sir Pexall Brocas failed to do this and the glebe, valued at 100 marks, was permanently
added to the manorial estate.[18] The Revd John Orpwood was rector from 1602 to 1658
but he supplemented his income in 1637 by the purchase of 60 a. of freehold land, which
in c.1670[19] passed to his son, who had succeeded him as rector in 1661, after a gap of
three years. In 1697 there was only 3 a. of glebe when the terrier of that year recorded,

8   HRO, 21M65/A1/29, f.8,13.
9   Ibid., 39M89/E/B76.
10   *Winchester Dioc.Year Book* (1941–2), 42-3.
11   *Crockfield Clerical Dir.* (1947), 547.
12   HRO, 71M82/PB3.
13   *Tax Eccl.*
14   *Nonarum Inquisitiones*, 120.
15   TNA, E 368/438.
16   Ibid., C 78/3/98.
17   *Acts of PC* (1591–2), 487–9.
18   TNA, STAC 8/8/11.
19   Ibid., C 6/49/54.

'There hath formerly been (by common fame) a great deal more gleib land belonging to the said Rectory, which lyeth dispersedly among the lands of the Lord of the Manor and hath been detained from the church beyond the memory of man, of which we can give no other account than by tradition.'[20]

In 1722 the right of the advowson and presentation to the parsonage was valued at £80 to £100 a year.[21] Rectors from the mid 18th century rented extra land to supplement their income. George Austen (1761–1805) and Cassandra, his wife, were granted a messuage and a 4 a. close for 2s. a year.[22] To further supplement his income, Revd George Austen also rented Cheesedown farm (200 a.).[23]

When the lord of the manor, Edward Knight appointed his son, William, as rector in 1823, he endowed the rectory with 50 a. of additional glebe land from Street farm.[24] Edward Knight also exchanged small pieces of land with his tenant, William Digweed, to facilitate this new endowment giving Knight 3 a. of meadow, a drove way and a cottage, which he could demolish, to enable him to grant all the area as glebe.[25] Knight obtained a licence from the Crown for the new glebe costing £275 arguing that a new house and additional glebe were needed to properly support a resident rector.[26] William Knight further increased his income by leasing from his father the remaining 40 a. of Street farm which comprised fields adjoining the glebe.[27] In 1851 the endowment consisted of tithe and glebe with the tithe commuted at £500. The rectory, garden and glebe occupied 56 a.[28] and were valued at £485 in 1859.[29] On Edward Knight's death in 1852, Street farm was leased to the Revd William Knight for life (60 years). The glebe and the 40 a. of Street farm were left out of the sale from his brother, Edward, to the second duke of Wellington at William's request.[30] The glebe and Street farm were offered to the duke of Wellington, and then to William. William Knight did not want to purchase the Street farm portion,[31] and continued to pay £30 a year rent to his brother for Street farm and £15 4s. 0d. rent for the cottages until 1860,[32] when Edward Knight apparently sold the rectory, glebe, the right of presentation to the living and the 43 a. of Street farm to the Revd Gilbert Alder, vicar of Vernham Dean and rector of Hurstbourne Tarrant.[33] This was inherited by the Revd Herbert Alder, whose brother, Edward, bought it in 1888 and was himself rector of

20   HRO, 21M65/E15/112.
21   Ibid., 39M89/E/B/639/1.
22   Ibid., 18M61/tin box C.
23   Austen, *Letters*, 54.
24   Jane Austen's House Museum, Chawton, Steventon Glebe Land Map (1821).
25   HRO, 18M61/box F/bundle 9. About 1 a. of this was not officially included in the new glebe but intermixed with it.
26   HRO, 18M61/box F/bundle 9.
27   Ibid., 21M65/F7/223/1.
28   *Rel. Census 1851*, 188.
29   *White's Dir. Hants. & IOW*, 1859, 514.
30   HRO, 39M89/E/T27.
31   Ibid.
32   Ibid., 18M61/box 85/bundle 3; 79M78/B213–4.
33   Ibid., 39M89/E/B76, 39M89/E/T26. *Alumni* Cantab. Part II, vol. I, 23. *VCH Hants.* IV, 174 stated the rectory was sold by the duke of Wellington to the Revd G. Alder but this is very unlikely as the land was not sold to the duke, but the sale documents from Knight to the Revd Gilbert Alder have not been discovered.

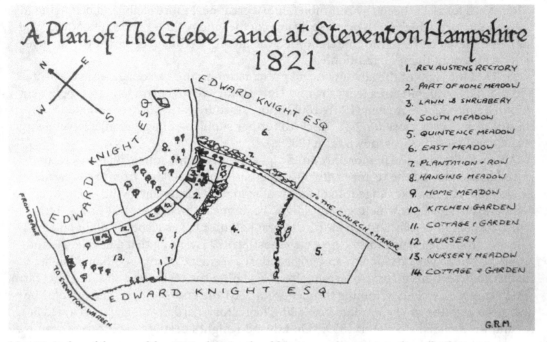

Map 13 *A plan of the new glebe, 1821, showing the old rectory and cottages in the valley bottom just before they were pulled down.*

Steventon until 1901.[34] The Alder family continued to own the rectory until 1930 when Steventon parish was united with North Waltham and the glebe and rectory were sold into private hands.[35]

Tithes

The tithe of cheese with oblations and mortuaries was worth £4 0s. 8d. in 1341.[36] In 1535–6 the rectory was valued at £11 4s. 4½d .[37] The great and small tithes seized by Sir Pexall Brocas were restored to the rectory with other fees.[38] The parish was inclosed in a piecemeal manner culminating in a private inclosure of the remnants of the open fields in c.1740 but the tithes were not commuted. Tithes of hay, lambs and wool were still paid in kind in 1743.[39] Tithes were negotiated in the early 18th century between the tenants of the Manor farm, William Parker and later William Hellier, and the incumbent. On the Revd Haddon's death in 1743 the tenants asked Thomas Knight to appoint a new rector who would not be extortionate in his demands.[40] The average net value of the benefice

34   HRO, 46M84/C27/2/1.
35   Ibid., 68M72/DDZ14.
36   *Nonarum Inquisitiones*, 120.
37   *Valor Eccl.*, II, 15.
38   HRO, 21M65/E15/112.
39   Ibid., 39M38/E/B622, 18M61/tin box C.
40   Ibid., 18M61/tin box C.

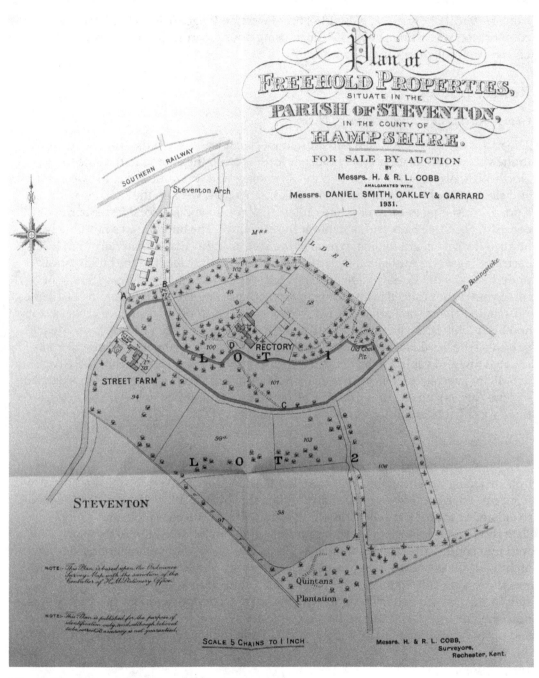

Map 14 *The glebe and Street Farm sold in 1930.*

from 1829 to 1831 was £485.[41] By 1838 tithes were no longer paid in kind and the average composition was estimated at £435 albeit using poor records; this was converted into a £500 a year rent charge in the same year.[42]

Rectory Houses

George Austen's Rectory/Parsonage House

The rectory (Fig. 24) in which Jane Austen was born was built in the late 15th century in the valley bottom at the end of the lane leading from the church to the lane to North Waltham. In 1697 it was a house of two bays and was outletted at the west end and along part of the south side over a cellar. Two barns were on the site: one with a porch consisting of three bays and outletted all round and a second lesser barn consisting of three bays, with a stable at the east end.[43] The building was most likely to be a rural vernacular building, typical of the area, using available materials from local surroundings. The Austen family letters state that refurbishment of the building was undertaken by the Revd George Austen before the couple and their young family of three young sons moved from Deane to Steventon in late 1768 (Fig. 24).[44] In 1801 James Austen, the eldest son (curate 1801–5, rector 1805–19), took up residence at the rectory and he and his family lived there until 1819. From January 1820 to 1823 the residence passed to the Revd Henry Austen, the fourth son. In 1824 the house was described as situated low and subject to be flooded and distant from the greater part of the village and in a dilapidated state.[45] Shortly before demolition the old rectory (Fig. 24) was sketched by Jane Austen's niece, Anna Lefroy. The house was demolished in 1824, and in 2015 there was no longer any visual trace of the building.

New Rectory 1823–4

Edward Knight built a new rectory (Fig. 22) for his son, William, in 1823–4 on the hillside facing the site of the old rectory but in a healthier place accessible by a drive from the Triangle. It was a gentleman's residence, which cost £5,500 to build, designed to enhance the comfort and status of the rector.[46] It had stucco walling and a hipped slate roof. Large sash windows with stone sills and plinths were set into its south-west and south-east fronts. It boasted a classical doorway with pediment brackets and architrave. To the north-west was a small wing with a single storey connecting link which was the former side entrance. There was a tall round-headed staircase window in the small wing.[47] It had two main floors with servants' accommodation in the attics. It was described in 1859 as a large and handsome rectory house with a finely wooded lawn and pleasure grounds.[48] In 1898 the house had stabling for six horses and a double coach

41 *Parl. Papers,* 1935, (67).
42 TNA, IR 18/9144.
43 HRO, 21M65/E15/112.
44 Jane Austen House Museum, Chawton, Steventon Rectory, drawing by Anna Lefroy, front view.
45 HRO, 18M61/box E/bundle 9. A report on a recent excavation of the site of the rectory will be published in 2016.
46 HRO, 18M61/box E/bundle 9; *White's Dir. Hants.* (1878), 582.
47 NHL no. 1167592, 'Steventon House': 17 June 2014.
48 *White's Dir. Hants. & IOW* (1859), 514.

house. The house was heated by a hot water boiler in the basement.[49] In 1922 the Revd Herbert Steedman (rector 1901–30) borrowed £84 from Queen Anne's bounty for repairs to the parsonage house and offices but it was still in poor decorative order in 1931.[50] The rectory was sold for £2,200 in 1931–2 with 53 a. of glebe, including 8 a. of pleasure grounds[51] and in 2015 it was a grade II listed private house (Fig. 22).[52]

Pastoral Care and Religious Life

The Middle Ages to the Reformation

Around 20 rectors are known before the Reformation.[53] The first references are to a Geoffrey who had debt problems but also wanted to study. In 1292 Geoffrey, rector of Steventon, was charged with a debt of two quarters of wheat to Adam de Northampton, merchant of Winchester and Petronella, his wife.[54] This is likely to be the same Geoffrey who in August 1301 was granted leave of study for three years,[55] and who, described as Geoffrey of Monteney, was alleged in 1305 to owe 11 marks and 6d. to Richard of Middelton.[56] Roger de Roches, kinsman of the patron, John de Roches, became rector in August 1307 but he had also been presented by the bishop (by lapse) in 1306 to Bradley, which led to a dispute in 1308, when John de Roches wanted to present John of Vienne to Bradley and Roger de Roches was challenged to show why he should hold two livings.[57] John de Pulburgh, deacon, was admitted and instituted as rector to the vacant church of Steventon in 1324 at the presentation of John de Roches.[58] John de Pulburgh was ordained priest in March 1325.[59] Many of the rectors were acolytes or sub-deacons when appointed. John de Insula was ordained sub-deacon in 1346 while rector of Steventon.[60] He was succeeded by Walter de Brockhampton, acolyte, in January 1349; he was ordained subdeacon and deacon in March 1349, and priest in April 1349, perhaps reflecting the shortage of priests after the Black Death.[61] In September 1375 John Chitterne (d. by 28 Apr. 1419),[62] rector of Steventon, with only the first clerical tonsure, was ordained acolyte.[63] Chitterne resigned and was succeeded by John Depynge in February 1376; he also had only his first clerical tonsure, and was given licence of non-residence in November 1376 for three years to study at Oxford or elsewhere and then ordained

49 HRO, 46M84/C27/6.
50 CE Rec. Centre, D377856.
51 HRO, 68M72 DDZ14.
52 NHL no. 1167592, 'Steventon House', 14 June 2014.
53 Episcopal registers for Winchester diocese survive from 1282–3.
54 TNA, C 241/22/87.
55 *Reg. Pontoise*, I, 113.
56 *Reg. Woodlock*, l. 897.
57 Ibid., 721, 726, 728. John de Roches was patron of both livings. The dispute was apparently decided in favour of John of Vienne who was ordained rector of Bradley in 1308.
58 *Reg. Stratford* I, 285, 862.
59 Ibid., II, 451, 1477.
60 *Reg. Edington*, part 1, 46–66, part 2, 106.
61 Ibid., part 1, 57; part 2, 138, 142, 144.
62 *Reg. Lacy (Heref.)*, 115; *Fasti Eccl. Sar.*, ed. Jones, 160.
63 *Reg. Wykeham*, I, 277.

Figure 22
*Rectory built 1824,
called Steventon House
from 1931.*

deacon.[64] In 1380 John Depynge was replaced in an exchange by Robert de Haytefeld.[65] In 1396 John Chitterne, by then a priest, was instituted at Steventon.[66] Between his stints at Steventon Chitterne was resident in London in 1392.[67] In 1391 and 1397 he was described as one of the clerks of Chancery and while presumably routinely absent from Steventon, was employed by the Brocas family; in the same year he launched an action against the executors of Sir Bernard Brocas for debt.[68] John resigned Steventon in 1399 but continued to be associated with the Brocas family and with chancery.[69] From the 1370s, he was party to conveyances of land across southern England from Wiltshire to Essex[70] and after 1400 held prebendaries and canonries in Wiltshire, Salisbury cathedral and Hereford, and at the time of his death, was archdeacon of Wiltshire.[71] John Stevens, priest, succeeded Chitterne[72] and was succeeded in June 1401 by Roland de Thornburgh,[73] who was

64   *Reg. Wykeham*, I, 75; II, 264.
65   Ibid., I, 105.
66   Ibid., I, 202.
67   For example, *Cal. Close*, 1385-1389, 98; A.K. McHardy, 'Ecclesiastical property in the City of London, 1392: Broad Street Ward', in *The Church in London 1375–1392* (1977), 49–50.
68   *Cal. Papal Regs, IV, 495, 99; Cal. Close*, 1396–99, 208.
69   See, for example: *Cal. Close*, 1405–09, 93; C. Given-Wilson et al. *Parliament Rolls of Medieval England* (Woodbridge, 2005), VIII, 516 (Receiver of petitions from England, Ireland, Wales and Scotland, with others, Nov. 1411).
70   For example, TNA, CP 25(1)/256/57, no. 25, *Cal. Close*, 1399–1402, 325 (Chicklade, Wilts.); *Cal. Close*. 1392–6, 358, 360.
71   *VCH Wilts.* III, 391–2; *Fasti Eccl. Sar.*, ed. Jones, 160; *Reg. Trefnant* (Heref.), 188; *Reg. Lacy* (*Heref.*), 115; *Cal. Pat.* 1416–22, 286.
72   *Reg. Wykeham*, I, 219.
73   Ibid., I, 233. A variation of this was Thornburge.

ordained deacon and then priest in February and March of 1402–3.[74] Thornburgh was succeeded in late March 1404 by Richard Scarburgh who in turn was replaced by John Colet in June of 1409.[75] There is a gap in the records in the early 15th century until John Baron was appointed in November 1451.[76] After this four rectors died while still in office. Thomas Herryson succeeded following the death of Baron in January 1467–8,[77] John Maxflete[78] succeeded him in 1472,[79] and Robert Fawley followed Maxflete in January 1481–2.[80] By 1517 John Wafer was rector and continued until his death in 1538, when he was succeeded by John Bennett, 1538–48.[81] Both were absentee rectors who employed curates.[82] After John Bennett's death, the rectory was vacant for a few years, with Richard Mills appointed by 1555.[83]

Immediately before the Reformation, Steventon was a traditional Catholic community in which testators paid for prayers for their souls in purgatory and for lights for the statues of the saints in St Nicholas Church. Care of souls was provided by curates in the 1520s and 1530s, such as Roger Sandeforth,[84] who also witnessed wills.[85] Christopher Denby (d. 1528) left the 20s. he owed to the curate to Sir Roger Sandford. Denby's will reflected his Catholic faith with his soul bequeathed to Almighty God, the blessed Saint Mary and to all the Company of Heaven.[86] Another seven testators from 1533 to 1559 bequeathed their souls to Almighty God, St Mary and the Company of Heaven.[87] Six testators[88] provided for prayers for their souls: John Waite (d. 1533) instructed his executors to provide bread, ale and cheese for the month mind (requiem mass celebrated one month after death) for himself and his wife, and for six masses to be said each year at St Nicholas for their souls.[89] Similarly, Joanne Morall (d. 1546) left five sheep to Sir Reginald Harrison, the curate,[90] to sing a trental of masses,[91] for the souls of herself, her husband and all Christian souls.[92] Her husband (d. 1546) left bequests to seven local churches with requests that they prayed for him.[93] Four testators from 1528 to 1533 left

74   *Reg. Wykeham,* I. 353-4.
75   Ibid., I, 245; Reg. Beaufort, ff. 24, 54.
76   Reg. Waynflete, I, f.39.
77   Ibid., I, f.157.
78   Variations of this name are Marflet and Marflete.
79   Reg. Waynflete, II, f.14b.
80   Ibid., II, f.87b.
81   HRO, 21M65/B1/1, Reg. Gardiner, f.36b.
82   TNA, C 78/3/98.
83   HRO, 21M65/B1/8.
84   Variants of this name include Sandford.
85   HRO, 21M65/B1/1-3.
86   Ibid., 1528B/14.
87   Ibid., 1533B/40, 1533B/38, 1533B/31, 1535B/34, 1546B/124, 1546B/125, 1559A/056.
88   Ibid., 1528B/14, 1533B/40, 1533B/38, 1559A/056.
89   Ibid., 1535B/34.
90   Ibid., 21M65/B1/5.
91   Which meant 30 masses on successive days.
92   HRO, 1546B/124.
93   Ibid., 1546B/125. The churches were Steventon, West Sherborne, Deane, Waltham, Tadley, Wolverton and Baughurst.

from one to three sheep each to maintain the lights in front of the images of St Nicholas, Our Lady and St Anthony.[94]

The Reformation to 2015

By 1568 the Reformation was evident. Wills bequeathed the soul to Almighty God and made no references to purgatory. Richard Mills continued as rector until his death in 1581, employing a curate for six of his last ten years in office.[95] He was succeeded from 1582 by Dr Ralph Thompson, a fellow of Brasenose College, Oxford, who was a chaplain to Elizabeth I, and also held the rectory of Settrington (Yorks.) from 1589 until his death in 1591.[96] Thompson spent time in Steventon in the early years of his ministry and employed a curate, but from 1587 to 1591 he did not appear for visitations and no curate was employed.[97] There were serious problems with ministry in the parish at this period. Sir Pexall Brocas, lord of the manor, had seized the rectorial tithes and glebe, closed the church and stopped divine service.[98] After Thompson's death, Sir Pexall was ordered first by the Court of Requests and subsequently by the Privy Council to pay Thompson's widow the rents and tithes which he had withheld from her.[99] Peter Sefton,[100] followed as rector from 1591 but his ministry and those of his two successors, John Browne (1595–6) and Henry Nelson (1598) a graduate of Pembroke College, Cambridge, who had been chaplain to the earl of Essex for nine years,[101] were impeded by Sir Pexall Brocas. Sir Pexall failed to pay Peter Sefton (1591–5) the £20 a year he offered him to be rector, so Sefton left and no church service was held for eight months. He treated John Browne and Henry Nelson in the same way, so both left and there was no divine service.[102] In 1605 Sir Edward Coke, attorney general, summed up Sir Pexall Brocas's alleged crimes against the church, rectors and parishioners of Steventon, stating that Sir Pexall had taken the glebe and tithes of the last three incumbents of Steventon rectory and taken all the crops to his own barns. One of his servants had locked the church for one month so no services had taken place. After the month, parishioners broke into the church for a baptism and the door was left open for three months, in which period cattle and sheep strayed in. In 1605 John Crook stated that Sir Pexall had not taken communion for 16 years.[103] The church was in a bad state of repair. Eventually in 1613 the archbishop of Canterbury excommunicated Sir Pexall Brocas.[104]

Meanwhile in 1602 John Orpwood, a Trinity College, Oxford MA, was presented by the bishop of Winchester[105] into the vacant rectory where he remained until his death in

94   HRO, 1528B/14, 1533B/40, 1533B/38, 1533B/34.
95   Ibid., 21M65/B1/11, 15.
96   *Alumni Oxon.*, 1500–1714, 1477. Variants of his name are Tompson, Tomson and Thomason.
97   HRO, 21M65/B1/15–19.
98   TNA, STAC 8/8/11.
99   *Acts of PC* (1591–2), 487–9.
100 HRO, 21M65/B1/20, 21. Sefton appeared at the episcopal visitation of 1592 at Basingstoke but although named as rector, did not attend the visitations in 1593–5.
101 *Alumni Cantab.* to 1751, 240.
102 TNA, STAC 8/87/3; HRO, 21M65/A1/28, f.4; 29, f.8.
103 TNA, STAC 8/8/11.
104 Ibid., STAC 8/82/3.
105 HRO, 21M65/A1/29, f. 13. *Alumni Oxon.*, 1500–1714, 1092.

1658.[106] Baptism and marriage records survive from 1604, burials from 1607, so Orpwood clearly held church services.[107] There were 40 communicants in 1603 with no Catholics or non-conformists.[108] John Orpwood, rector, was buried 11 December 1658, before which date his son alleged that he had become insane and because of this did not make a will.[109] Who cared for the parishioners in Orpwood's latter years was not recorded. He was succeeded on 31st December 1658 by Francis Clerke,[110] a Parliamentarian appointment with Richard Evelyn as patron and certificates from Stephen Webb of Basingstoke, John Brocket of Bentworth, Martin Morland of Cliddesden and John Marriot of Upper Wallop. In 1661 at the Restoration John Orpwood, a graduate of St Edmund Hall, Oxford,[111] son of the earlier John Orpwood (d. 1658), was appointed rector with no reference to Clerke's fate. John Orpwood was also inducted into Ewhurst, from which John Harmar had been evicted, which he held in plurality until 1664.[112] The religious community had expanded by 1676 to 53 communicants.[113] John Orpwood, like his father, apparently suffered from senility in later life causing the lord of the manor, John Lewknor, and the parishioners to petition the bishop of Winchester in 1694 for a new rector during the 'second childhood' of the minister.[114] He was briefly followed by Richard Deane, a graduate of Queen's College, Oxford, from 1695 to 1697[115] and then by Thomas Church (d. 1720) from 1697 to 1720.[116] Richard Wright was rector from 1720 to 1727, when there were about 80 parishioners. He reported that there were no chapels, lecturers, curates, dissenters or papists.[117] A schedule attached to the glebe terrier of 1728 shows traditional equipment for communion and services in the church, including a silver chalice, surplice, bible, common prayer book, three bells and a chest.[118] The next rectors were John Church, son of Thomas Church (d. 1720),[119] from 1727 to his death in 1733, David Strachan (1733–7) and Henry Haddon (1737–43) followed[120]. Haddon died in 1743 and was succeeded by William Payne, MA, a fellow of Magdalen College, Oxford,[121] who was apparently appointed to fill the post until Haddon's son was old enough to assume it. William Payne expressed concern about his appointment to the lord of the manor, Thomas Knight, wondering if he would be allowed to resign and stating that the bishop of Salisbury had opposed a resignation. Payne appears to have resigned but then

106 HRO, 71M82/PR1.
107 Ibid.
108 *Dioc. Pop. Rtns*, 490.
109 TNA, C 5/533/1.
110 LPL COMM III/7 p. 166. Clerke may be the same Francis Clerke, who in Apr. 1665, was inducted as rector of Stoke d'Alberon/Awborne, Surrey, also Winchester dioc., HRO, 21M65/F1/2, A1/33.
111 *Alumni Oxon.1500-1714*, 1092.
112 HRO, 35M48/5/1; http://db.theclergydatabase.org.uk/jsp/locations/index.jsp (accessed 2 Feb. 2015).
113 *Compton Census*, 85. The question was slightly different in 1676 asking how many in the parish were of an age to take communion.
114 HRO, 18M61/box 80/bundle 36.
115 Ibid., 1697B/13. *Alumni Oxon. 1500–1714*, 390.
116 HRO, 1720B/10.
117 *Parson and Parish*, 127.
118 HRO, 35M48/16/375.
119 Ibid., 1733B/15.
120 Ibid., 35M48/5/1.
121 Ibid., 21M65/E4/4/29.

been inducted a second time.[122] Payne was succeeded by Stephen Abthorpe until 1759 from which date for over 100 years members of the Austen/Knight family, all related to the lords of the manor, held the living. The first to be appointed was Henry Austen in 1754 and when he resigned in 1761 the lord of the manor, Thomas Knight, appointed Henry's cousin, George Austen, an Oxford graduate, as rector. Henry and George Austen were distant cousins of Knight's wife. George Austen remained in Oxford initially leaving the curate, Thomas Bathurst, appointed in 1754, to run the parish.[123] After marrying Cassandra Leigh, George Austen lived in Deane parsonage while Steventon rectory was modernized, only moving into Steventon in 1769, six years before his daughter, Jane Austen, was born. In 1765 two services were held each Sunday and communion was held at least three times a year.[124] In 1798 James Digweed, son of Hugh Digweed, tenant of Manor farm, was curate of Steventon having recently been ordained deacon and priest by the bishop of Winchester.[125] From 1801 to 1805 George Austen lived in Bath while his son, James Austen, ran the parish as curate and resided in the rectory. From 1791 James had also been vicar of Sherborne St John. He became rector of Steventon when his father died in 1805.[126] In 1810 James Austen held Steventon (population 150) and Sherborne St John (population 400), six miles apart. He lived in Steventon and held services in both parishes.[127] He was succeeded by his brother, Henry, from 1820 to 1823, followed by his nephew, William Knight, graduate of Exeter College, Oxford, who was rector for 50 years from 1823 to 1873. William Knight at times employed a curate: James Digweed was curate in 1829 and Francis Robinson in 1830 at a stipend of £80.[128] Under William Knight religious buildings and land in the parish were transformed: the church was restored with a new roof, tower and spire and a new rectory was built with an endowment of 50 a. of additional glebe. In 1851 the church could accommodate 150 worshippers. On the morning of the census (30th March) 52 adults attended church with 51 present in the evening. Fifteen children went to Sunday school in the morning and sixteen in the evening.[129] The rector's duties comprised one full morning service and afternoon (evening) prayers each Sunday.[130]

Herbert Alder, graduate of Trinity Hall, Cambridge, was rector from 1874 to 1886;[131] by 1885 Alder lived at Trinity Hall, Cambridge and Richard Arthur Walls was curate in charge (1884–6).[132] Henry C. D. Chandler was then rector (1886–9) with N.E. Willoughby as curate.[133] From 1889 to 1901 Edward Alder of Trinity Hall, Cambridge, but resident in the rectory in 1891, was rector with no curate.[134] The last rector of Steventon as an independent parish was Herbert Edward Watson Steedman who was appointed in

122 HRO, 39M89/E/B559/3, 21M65/A2/1, 35M48/6/528, 547.
123 *Family Record*, 6.
124 HRO, 21M65/B4/2/77.
125 *Doing the Duty*, 38.
126 HRO, 21M65/E2/845.
127 *Doing the duty*, 99, 108.
128 HRO, 21M65/B1/154, E6/1.
129 *Relig. Census* 1851, 188.
130 HRO, 39M89/E/B76.
131 *Alumni Cantab. 1752–1900*, 23; *Crockford's Clerical Dir.* (1877), 8; (1889), 11.
132 *Kelly's Dir. Hants.* (1885), 971.
133 *Crockford's Clerical Dir.* (1889), 1727.
134 Census 1891, *Kelly's Dir. Hants.* (1895), 519–20.

1901.[135] Steedman served, holding services every Sunday, until the parish was merged with North Waltham in 1930, when he moved to Abbotts Ann parish.[136] Charles R. Hall, the rector of North Waltham,[137] also became the rector of Steventon on 9 April 1930,[138] and ministered from 1930 to 1947, without a curate, until he retired to a diocesan job in Portsmouth.[139] In 1935 a service was held every Sunday morning with Communion preceding it once a month. Evening services also took place twice a month.[140] Concerns were expressed by the Parochial Church Council to the patron, the Martyrs' Memorial Trust, after Hall's departure about falling church attendance and the impact of treating the benefice as a retirement post and church attendance was described as 'lamentably low'.[141] Louis A. Bralant was a relatively young rector from 1948 to 1950 but then moved to London.[142] He was succeeded by Colin J. Thompson, who remained until 1959, holding services every Sunday morning and evening but attendance at any service rarely exceeded 20 and sometimes fell under 10.[143] The rectory was vacant in 1959–60, with concern again expressed about falling church attendance and the need for a younger rector to attract young people with a youth club, Guides and Scouts, rather than viewing it as a 'pleasant semi-retirement post'.[144] Nonetheless William B. Norris, rector (1961–74), was in his mid 50s when appointed[145] and Geoffrey R. Turner was rector of Steventon, North Waltham, Ashe and Deane from 1976 until his death in 1992.[146] Michael S. Kenning was rector of North Waltham, Steventon, Ashe and Deane from 1992 until his retirement in 2010; he was also rural dean of Whitchurch from 2003 to 2008, honorary canon of Winchester Cathedral from 2009 and well known for his studies of, and talks about, Jane Austen.[147] From 2011 Ian Smale, priest in charge of St Mary, Overton, was overall priest in charge of the benefice including Steventon with the Revd Julia Foster, based at the Rectory, North Waltham, having special responsibility for Steventon parish.[148] In 2015 services in Steventon were only held on every fourth Sunday. Regular services were held each Sunday in the neighbouring parish of North Waltham.[149]

135 *Crockford's Clerical Dir.* (1903), 1924.
136 HRO, 35M48/6/3062; 71M82PI1.
137 Ibid., 35M48/6/3057.
138 LPL, N6704.
139 *Crockford's Clerical Dir.* (1933), 545; HRO, 71M82/PB5.
140 Ibid., 71M82/PI1.
141 Ibid., 71M82/PB5.
142 *Crockford's Clerical Dir.* (1949–50), 1758.
143 Ibid. (1955-6), 1155; HRO, 71M82/PI1.
144 Ibid., 71M82/PB5.
145 *Crockford's Clerical Dir.* (1963–4), 893. Norris was rector of North Waltham, Steventon and Dummer from 1961–72 and then of North Waltham, Steventon, Ashe and Deane.
146 *Crockford's Clerical Dir.* (1991–2), 728; HRO, 15M76/PW10.
147 http://www.janeaustensoci.freeuk.com/pages/conference_speakers.htm (accessed 30 Jan. 2015). Crockford's Clerical Dir. (2010), 468.
148 *Crockford's Clerical Dir.*, http://www.crockford.org.uk (accessed 30 Jan. 2015).
149 Local inf.

Church Room (Village Hall from 1979)

Pastoral care was enhanced following the merger of Steventon parish and the sale of
the glebe and rectory house, by the construction of a church or parish room (Fig. 20) in
1932, designed for dual use for religious services and as a social centre.[150] A plot of 510
sq. yards, on the site of Street Farm[151] and adjacent to the Triangle was excluded from
the rectory sale. £1,200 from the profits of the sale was used for building the room and
for seating and other fixtures. The architect was W. J. Carpenter Turner of Overton,
who later became Winchester cathedral architect.[152] The hall was built by Milsom & Son
of Basingstoke. The rector, Charles Hall, argued that religious services in the church
room were needed as the parish church was one mile from the village, with inadequate
light and heating. Alternate Sunday evening services were held in the sanctuary (10ft x
6ft 6in) which, together with the vestry, could be shut off when the room was used for
secular purposes. The sanctuary was equipped with a communion table and rails. Hall
also purchased six dozen chairs, a small table and two trestle tables, candlesticks, vases,
a cross, pews and a prayer desk, lectern, kneelers, hassocks, sanctuary carpet, vestry
chair, offertory plate, service books and curtains. The room was not intended to replace
the parish church and divine service would be held there every other Sunday afternoon
in winter with a service for children on another Sunday afternoon but morning service
would be held each Sunday in the church. The Sunday school was held in the room in the
1930s.[153] One of the parishioners loaned a harmonium organ. The social centre included
facilities for tea making so it could be a venue for fundraising meetings, designed to
raise money to pay for repairs to the church roof. The centre seated 103 people and
had hot water radiators and lighting.[154] The church room was opened in October 1932
by Mrs Onslow Fane and dedicated by the bishop of Southampton, Right Revd Cecil
Boutflower.[155] The church room was initially successful in both its uses. However, in 1943
Carpenter Turner complained to the archdeacon of Winchester that the rector had made
very little use of the church room and had quarrelled with the owner of the big house
who had built an alternative hall, further reducing the use of the church room! The
rector wanted to sell the church room which shocked the Ecclesiastical Commissioners
so soon after it had been built and after so much had been made by the same rector of
the need for nearer and more comfortable winter services.[156] Services did not survive in
the room and in 1976 it was deconsecrated but it continued as a social centre, renamed
the Village Hall (1979).[157]

150 LPL, ECE/7/1/84906.
151 HRO, 68M72/DDZ14.
152 See for example, HRO, 21M65/210F/16, dated 2 Aug. 1933.
153 Ibid., 71M83/PW3.
154 LPL, ECE/7/1/84906.
155 *Basingstoke Gaz.,* 7 Oct. 1932.
156 LPL, ECE/7/1/84906.
157 See p. 65.

The Church of St Nicholas[158]

An early ecclesiastical focus in the area is suggested by a surviving fragment of a late 8th-
or early 9th-century cross-shaft, reused in the Pexall manor house but now displayed
below the pulpit in the church.[159] The building of the church, a small and simple building
(Fig. 6), with aisleless nave and a smaller and narrower chancel, dates from about 1200.
It saw substantial remodelling in about the 15th century and major Victorian restoration
including the rebuilding of the west end and the addition of tower and spire (Figs 6 and
26).

This original church incorporates two finely cut lancet windows in the nave, and two
on each side in the chancel. The quoins show the use of lines of several blocks of ashlar
and thus of a relatively extravagant use of the imported stone. The basic structure of the
standing walls has remained, but at various times the appearance and details have been
changed. Significant rebuilding occurred in the late Middle Ages. Two at least of the nave
windows date from around the 15th century and seem to have been original, with the
other two probably Victorian insertions. The east main window also seems to have been
15th century, but was partly restored by 1911, and replaced in 1975.[160] During restoration
work in 1988, a medieval painting of a bishop saint was uncovered (Fig. 23).

Geoffrey Smith (d. 1533) left 1,000 shingles to the church to be purchased by his
executor.[161] Many 16th-century and early 17th-century testators left sheep or cash for the
maintenance and repair of St Nicholas church and often some of the surrounding parish
churches.[162] After 1616 in the surviving wills, such bequests were less frequent. The
church was in a very poor state of repair in 1605, with parts allegedly likely to fall down
on the parishioners' heads for want of maintenance.[163] In 1696 the church again needed
repairs.[164] At some time, probably in the later Middle Ages, a timber bell tower was built
at the west end within the shell of the church. This 'steeple' was a timber-framed bell
tower so typical of those being built in the small country churches around, and such
as still survives at Mapledurwell.[165] It was a square tower of boarded timber work that
projected from the main roof, and was capped by a pyramidal roof above. The tower was
in need of repair in 1733 and was being repaired in 1738.[166] The church was reported to
be very much out of repair in 1743 with only £62 spent on it in the 40 years that William
Parker had been tenant of the Manor farm and responsible for the church repairs.[167] By
1764 the church was in a very poor state and the steeple was blown down in high winds,
causing some damage to the roof of the church.[168]

158 See also *Pevsner North Hampshire*, 498–9.
159 D. Tweedle, M. Biddle and B. Kjϕlbe-Biddle, *Corpus of Anglo-Saxon Stone Sculpture* IV, *S.E. England*
     (1993), 37, 267–8.
160 *VCH Hants.* IV, 173; Pevsner, *North Hampshire*, 498.
161 HRO, 1533B/31.
162 See for example, Richard Ayliffe, HRO, 1572B/005; John Crooke, HRO, 1616B/028.
163 TNA, STAC 8/8/11.
164 HRO, 202M85/3/1125.
165 *Mapledurwell,* figure 20, 77.
166 HRO, 21M65/B2/762, 763.
167 Ibid., 18M61/tin box C.
168 Ibid.

Figure 23
Medieval painting of a bishop saint, uncovered during restoration work on the church in 1988.

It was the upper parts that were in great decay and, as a late 18th- or early 19th-century painting (Fig. 26) shows, no attempt had been made to restore the fallen tower. Instead the bells were rehung within the roof space with sound vent or openings into the roofline made to reduce any muffling effect of this lower closed location.[169] Of the three bells, one was 15th century, *c.*1470, another of 1670 and a third of unknown date.[170]

Something of the medieval arrangements survived, in a double piscina in the chancel and 13th-century wall paintings. Later internal rearrangements are reflected in the early 17th-century lord's pew: a timber inclosure, originally at the south-east corner of the nave but moved *c.*1914 to the west of the church, where it serves as a vestry.[171]

The church was heavily restored in the mid 19th century although probably in a succession of campaigns, commissioned by William Knight, rector (1823–73) (Figs.

169 This painting of the church before restoration is in the Sumner collection in Winchester cathedral (HRO, CD 34, 3A12-4). This image postdates the collapse of the steeple in 1764 and predates 1849 but cannot be dated exactly.
170 W.E. Colchester, *Hampshire Church Bells: their founders and inscriptions* (1920), 100.
171 HRO, 110M98/2.

Figure 24 *The old rectory where Jane Austen was born, sketched by her niece, Anna Lefroy, c.1820.*

6 and 26). Work was underway in 1835.[172] The chancel was rebuilt about 1844[173] and in 1849, William Dyer of Alton was commissioned to transform the west end with a stone tower and two new side windows. The spire was not yet included in the surviving drawings.[174] The spire probably represented a rethink during the building programme, since the tower was not given the full proposed height shown in the surviving drawings. Further activity occurred in 1864 when 'the entire church was restored'.[175] The font is dated 1868 and may represent William Knight's final action in the church. During this prolonged period of activity, the nave roof was entirely replaced, the chancel was also reroofed, with plaster, timber ribs and bosses, and the upper part of the chancel wall rebuilt.[176]

Elaborate internal decoration was painted on the chancel arch. Later changes included a painting of the Transfiguration over the chancel arch by C. E. Gray (1889) and the east window was restored by 1911 (Fig. 25). A small pipe organ was installed in 1912. Restoration work on the church roof and spire was completed in 1934 after an appeal which raised £676, of which £117 was paid by the Ecclesiastical Commissioners but the rest was raised by local appeals, including a donation of £100 from Mrs Onslow Fane.[177]

172 *Pevsner, North Hampshire,* 498.
173 *White's, Dir. Hants. & IOW* (1859), 514; (1878 edn) 582.
174 HRO, 18M61/box G/bundle 6, This also shows that Dyer also built a new barn at Cheesedown.
175 *White's, Dir. Hants. & IOW* (1878), 582.
176 Ibid. (1859), describes the chancel having been rebuilt 15 years before.
177 *Kelly's Dir. Hants.* (1935), 518; LPL ECE/7/1/84906; HRO, 41M64/PZ5.

Figure 25 *Interior of the church, 2014, showing the chancel arch and the painting of the Transfiguration (dated 1889).*

Figure 26 *St Nicholas church, Steventon, before the Victorian restoration and as Jane Austen saw it.*

A bronze tablet to the memory of Jane Austen was erected on the north wall of the nave in 1936.[178] The church roof and spire were restored in 1984, following an appeal set up in spring 1983.[179] The church benefits from its links with Jane Austen: in 1995, for example, the Jane Austen Society of North America financed some of the £5,000 renovation and retuning of the three bells, by church bellhangers Whites of Appleton, Oxfordshire.[180]

Methodism (Primitive and Union)

The only recorded example of nonconformity in Steventon was Methodism in the 20th century. A Primitive Methodist chapel was built in 1903 (Fig. 27) as part of the Micheldever Primitive Methodist circuit. Missionary meetings were held in Steventon from 1900 before the chapel was built.[181] In June 1901 Micheldever circuit approached Henry Harris, lord of the manor, regarding the purchase of land for the chapel.[182] From 1903 to 1973 services were held in a small Methodist chapel, built south of the Triangle, set back from Steventon Lane.[183] The land to build the chapel was purchased for £1 from Henry Harris with the proviso that the land and buildings should be sold back to the original vendor or his successor for £1 should the chapel cease to be used for

178 HRO, 71M82/PW5.
179 Steventon PCC, *The Church of St Nicholas Steventon* (2013).
180 HRO, 71M82/PW13/1–44.
181 Ibid., 96M72/NMC/B48.
182 Ibid.
183 Ibid., 69A04/A4.

Figure 27 *Steventon Primitive Methodist Chapel (a tin tabernacle) featuring a rally of the Women's Own, 1938.*

worship.[184] The chapel was built, at a cost of £150, of corrugated iron, with a wooden lining and initially lit by oil lamps with music provided by a small harmonium.[185] The first trustees, selected at a meeting in John Beck's cottage in Steventon, were John Beck, shepherd; Henry Dyer, shepherd; Richard Harding, signalman; James Moore, labourer; Albert Kersley, carter and Charles Sharpe, farmer, with five others from surrounding chapels.[186] In 1904, there were 24 scholars in the Sunday school, held in the chapel on Sunday afternoons, and 24 adult temperance members, and a Band of Hope (20 members) who were juvenile abstainers.[187] In 1907 45 people attended the services on Sundays.[188] But enthusiasm for the Sunday school waned and, by 1910, it had only 9 pupils, finally closing in 1912. In 1919 the chapel had 20 members, rising to 30 for most of the 1920s but then falling to 5 members by 1930.[189] The Sunday school was revived in 1928 with 11 pupils, rising to 29 in 1931, a year in which Micheldever circuit claimed progress among scholars despite 'modern forms of temptation … and in some schools, the influence of Parish Priests'.[190] From the 1930s to the 1960s Mrs Agnes Titheridge (d.1977) ran the Sunday school and was also a Methodist local preacher.[191] In Britain, the

---

184 HRO, 96M72/NMS/D87.
185 Le Faye, *Steventon,* 52. HRO, 96M72/NMC/B52.
186 HRO, 96M72/NMC/B44.
187 Ibid., 96M72/NMC/B52.
188 Ibid., 96M72/NMC/B53.
189 Ibid.
190 Ibid., 96M72/NMC/B52.
191 North Waltham, Steventon, Ashe and Deane parish magazine, Mar. 1977.

Methodist Church was formed in 1932 from three separate Methodist denominations: the Wesleyan, Primitive and United Methodist churches. Different Methodist groups slowly joined the Methodist union. In Steventon the Primitive Methodists became part of this united Methodist church in 1948 when the Micheldever circuit merged with the Andover and Hurstbourne circuits to form the Andover Trinity Methodist circuit which, after merger with the Andover East Street Primitive Circuit, became the Andover circuit in 1951.[192] An organ was installed in the chapel in 1948 and electric lighting in 1953.[193] Services were held every Sunday by a minister from the Methodist circuit or a licensed local preacher. Funds were very limited with, at most, £30 collected in any one year and in some years only £10.[194] The congregation was small with only two baptisms of Steventon Methodists recorded from 1934 to 1973.[195] The church was managed by lay members: in 1955 Mrs Titheridge was secretary and treasurer, Mrs Rogers was caretaker, Mr Titheridge was chapel steward and Philip Bolton was organist. Members also painted the building, but this was in poor repair by 1971 and repair costs were judged to exceed the trust fund.[196] Despite a visitation and an evangelical campaign, services ceased in 1973, when the chapel had only seven members who transferred to North Waltham, one mile away.[197] The building and land was then sold to the lord of the manor, Mr Angus Mackinnon of Sutton Scotney, for £1.[198]

192 HRO, 96M72.
193 Ibid., 96M72/NMS/D86.
194 Ibid.
195 Ibid., 96M72/NMR26.
196 Ibid., 96M72/NMS/D85.
197 Ibid, 96M72/NMS/D87.
198 Ibid.

ABBREVIATIONS

Abbreviations and short titles used include the following:

a.	acre(s)
Acts of PC	*Acts of the Privy Council of England* (HMSO, 1890–1964)
Agrarian Hist. England, 4	Joan Thirsk (ed.), *The Agrarian History of England and Wales*, 4 (Cambridge, 1967)
Alumni Cantab. to 1751 or 1752–1900	J. Venn and J.A. Venn, *Alumni Cantabrigienses*, Parts 1 and 2 (Cambridge, 1922–27 and 1940–54)
Alumni Oxon.	J. Foster, (ed.) *Alumni Oxoniensis* 1500–1714 and 1752–1900
Archaeol. Jnl	*Archaeological Journal*
Austen, *Letters*	D. Le Faye (ed.), *Jane Austen's Letters*, (3rd edn, Oxford, 1995)
Austen-Leigh, *Memoir*	James Edward Austen-Leigh, *A Memoir of Jane Austen*, (5th ed., London, 1883)
Austen Papers	R.A. Austen Leigh (ed.) *Austen Papers 1704–1856* (London, 1942)
Baigent and Millard, *Basingstoke*	F.J. Baigent and J.E. Millard, *A History of the Ancient Town and Manor of Basingstoke in the County of Southampton with a Brief Account of the Siege of Basing House, A.D. 1643–1645* (Basingstoke, 1889)
Besse, *Sufferings*	J. Besse, *A Collection of the Sufferings of the People called Quakers, from 1650 to 1689* (London, 1753)
BL	British Library
Burrows, *Brocas*	M. Burrows, *The Family of Brocas of Beaurepaire and Roche Court; Hereditary Masters of the Royal Buckhounds; with Some Account of the English Rule in Aquitaine*, London, 1886
Calamy Revised	A.G. Matthews (ed.), *Calamy Revised*, (Oxford, 1934)
Cal. Chart.	*Calendar of the Charter Rolls preserved in the Public Record Office* (HMSO, 1903–27)

Cal. Close	*Calendar of the Close Rolls preserved in the Public Record Office* (HMSO, 1892–1963)
Cal. Cttee for Compounding	*Calendar of the Proceedings of the Committee for Compounding, etc.* (HMSO, 1889–92)
Cal. Inq. Misc.	*Calendar of Inquisitions Miscellaneous (Chancery) preserved in the Public Record Office* (HMSO, 1916–68)
Cal. Inq. p.m.	*Calendar of Inquisitions post mortem preserved in the Public Record Office* (HMSO, 1904–87)
Cal. Pat.	*Calendar of the Patent Rolls preserved in the Public Record Office* (HMSO, 1890–1986)
Cal. S.P. Dom.	*Calendar of State Papers, Domestic Series* (HMSO, 1856–1972)
CCCO	Corpus Christi College, Oxford
CE Rec. Centre	Church of England Record Centre, South Bermondsey, London
CH	Copyhold
Char. Com.	Charity Commission
Close	*Close Rolls of the Reign of Henry III preserved in the Public Record Office* (HMSO, 1902–15)
Collins, *Parson's Daughter*	I. Collins, *The Parson's Daughter* (London, 1998)
Compton Census	A. Whiteman (ed.), *The Compton Census of* 1676 (Records of Social and Economic History, n.s. 10, 1986)
Crockford Clerical Dir.	*Crockford's Clerical Directory*
Dioc. Pop. Rtns	A. Dyer and D.M. Palliser (eds), *Diocesan Population Returns for 1563 and 1603* (Records of Social and Economic History, n.s. 31, 2005)
Doing the Duty	Mark Smith (ed.), *Doing the Duty of the Parish: Surveys of the Church in Hampshire 1810* (HRS 17, 2004)
Dir.	*Directory*
Domesday Book	A. Martin and G.H. Martin (eds), *Domesday Book: A Complete Translation* (London, 2002)
Excerpta e Rot. Finium	*Excerpta e Rotulis Finium,* Hen. III (Record Commission, 1835–6)
Family Record	D. Le Faye (ed.), *Jane Austen: A Family Record* (London, 1989)

Feudal Aids	*Inquisitions and Assessments relating to Feudal Aids preserved in the Public Record Office* (HMSO, 1899–1920)
Grover, *Hyde*	C. Grover, *Hyde: From Dissolution to Victorian Suburb* (Winchester, 2012)
Ha.	hectare(s)
Hampshire Treasures, 2	*Hampshire Treasures Survey, vol. 2 Basingstoke and Deane,* (Winchester, 1979)
Hants. Tax List, 1327	P. Mitchell-Fox and M. Page (eds)*The Hampshire Tax List of 1327* (HRS 20, 2014)
HCC	Hampshire County Council
HCU	Hampshire Congregational Union
Hearth Tax	E. Hughes and P. White (eds), *The Hampshire Hearth Tax Assessment 1665* (HRS 11, 1991)
HER	Historic Environment Record Hants.
Hist. Parl. Commons	*The History of Parliament. The House of Commons* (The History of Parliament Trust)
HRO	Hampshire Record Office
HRS	Hampshire Record Society before 1914; thereafter Hampshire Record Series
LPL	Lambeth Palace Library
L&SWR	London & South Western Railway
The lay subsidy of 1334	R.E. Glasscock (ed.)*The lay subsidy of 1334* (London, 1975)
Lay Subsidy	C.R. Davey (ed.), *The Hampshire Lay Subsidy Rolls, 1586* (HRS 4, 1981)
Le Faye, *Steventon*	D. Le Faye, *Jane Austen's Steventon* (Chawton, 1997)
m.	metre(s)
Manning and Bray, *The history … Surrey*, III	O. Manning and W. Bray, *The history and antiquities of the county of Surrey*, III (London, 1814, repr. 1974)
Mapledurwell	John Hare, Jean Morrin and Stan Waight, *The Victoria History of Hampshire: Mapledurwell* (London, 2012)
MERL	Museum of English Rural Life, Reading
Mun.	Muniments
NHL	National Heritage List for England (https://www.historicengland.org.uk/listing/the-list)

ODNB	*Oxford Dictionary of National Biography* (http://www.oxforddnb.com)
OS	Ordnance Survey
OS ABRC	OS Archaeology Branch Record Cards
Parl. Papers	*Parliamentary Papers*
Parson and Parish	W.R. Ward (ed.), *Parson and Parish in Eighteenth-Century Hampshire: Relies to Bishops' Visitations* (HRS 13, 1995)
PCC	Parochial church council
Pevsner, *North Hampshire*	M. Bullen, J. Crook, R. Hubbuck and N. Pevsner (eds), *Hampshire: Winchester and the North* (London, 2010)
Plac. de Quo Warr	*Placita de Quo Warranto* (Record Commission, 1818)
Proc. Hants. F.C.	*Proceedings of Hampshire Field Club*
Queen's Coll. Mun.	Muniments of The Queen's College, Oxford
Red Book Exch.	H. Hall (ed.), *Red Book of the Exchequer* (Rolls Series, 1896)
Regional distribution of wealth, 1524–5	J. Sheail, (ed. R.W. Hoyle) *The Regional Distribution of Wealth in England as Indicated in the 1524–5 Lay Subsidy Returns* (List and Index Society, special series, 28, Richmond, 1998)
Reg. Beaufort	HRO, 21M65/A1/12: register of Henry, Cardinal Beaufort, 1405–25
Reg. Edington	S.F. Hockey (ed.), *The Register of William Edington Bishop of Winchester, 1346–1366*, 2 vols (HRS 7 and 8, 1986–7)
Reg. Gardiner	HRO, 21M65/A/23 register of Stephen Gardiner, 1531–50
Reg. Pontoise	*Registrum Johannis de Pontissara*, vols 1 and 11 transcribed and edited by Cecil Deedes, Canterbury and York Society, vols 19 (1915), 30 (1918)
Reg. Stratford	*The Register of John de Stratford, Bishop of Winchester, 1323–1333, vol. I* (Surrey Record Society, 42, 2010)
Reg. Waynflete	HRO, 21M65/A1/13-14: register of William Waynflete i–ii, 1447–1486
Reg. Woodlock	A.W. Goodman (ed.), *Registrum Henrici Woodlock, Diocesis Wintoniensis, A.D. 1305–1316*, 2 vols. (Oxford, 1940–1)

Reg. Wykeham   T.F. Kirby (ed.), *Wykeham's Register*, i & ii (HRS, 1896–9)

Rel. Census 1851   J.A. Vickers, *The Religious Census 1851* (HRS 12, 1993)

Roberts, *Hampshire Houses*   E. Roberts, *Hampshire Houses, 1250–1700: Their Dating and Development* (Winchester, 2003)

Rot. Hund.   *Rotuli Hundredorum* (Record Commission, 2 volumes, 1812 and 1818)

Regs. Sandale & Asser   F.J. Baigent (ed.), *John de Sandale and Rigaud de Asserio AD 1316–1325. Episcopal Registers: Diocese of Winchester* (HRS, Winchester, c.1897)

Tanner, *Steventon*   R. Tanner, *Steventon – Jane Austen's Birthplace* (2008)

TNA   The National Archives

Valor Eccl.   *Valor Ecclesiasticus* (6 vols Record Commission, London, 1810–34)

VCH Hants.   *The Victoria History of the Counties of England: Hampshire and the Isle of Wight* (original editions, London, 1902–11)

Vincent, *Acta*   N. Vincent, *English Episcopal Acta: IX, Winchester 1205–38* (1994)

Walker Revised   A.G. Matthews (ed.) *Walker Revised* (Oxford, 1948)

WCM   Winchester College Muniments

WI   Women's Institute

Youngs, *Admin. Units*, 1   F.A. Youngs, *Guide to the Local Administrative Units of England, Vol.1, Southern England* (1979)

CPSIA information can be obtained
at www.ICGtesting.com
Printed in the USA
FSHW020535310321
79947FS